"Lanier has given us a biblical
ity that few if any have taken such an effort to form. The thoroughness of his research throughout Scripture leaves little doubt that his surprising conclusions are on solid ground. Describing biblical humility as 'aggression for God' as seen in the life of Christ raises the bar of understanding that most of us have never considered. This is a book you will use often in ministry."
> —**Peter Deison**, Associate Pastor, Park Cities Presbyterian Church, Dallas

"In a global culture consumed with the powerful and accomplished, Lanier Burns's careful study of humility and pride helps reorient our social assumptions with deep biblical thought. Sweeping from Genesis to the New Testament exemplars of the Lord Jesus Christ and the apostle Paul, Burns urges believers to true humility in an engaged, God-centered life—a way of life that he well exemplifies."
> —**J. Scott Horrell**, Professor of Theological Studies, Dallas Theological Seminary

"Too often we Christians exhibit pride in our interactions with others, both in the church and outside. Lanier Burns reminds us through a careful exposition of a host of biblical passages that humility is the way of our Lord Jesus Christ. This book not only informs us but, through a careful study of Scripture, leads to our personal transformation."
> —**Tremper Longman III**, Distinguished Scholar of Biblical Studies, Westmont College

"Dr. Lanier Burns, along with Dr. Howard Hendricks, has been one of the most sought-after professors at Dallas Theological Seminary. His integrity, his spiritual maturity, and his biblical insight make him more than qualified to pen *Pride and Humility at War*. I am honored to call him a friend—one whom I've known since I was in his wedding over fifty years ago. While his professional and academic credentials are without question, I would like to commend him to you as one who genuinely practices what he preaches—with humility."

—**Anne Graham Lotz**, Author, *The Daniel Prayer*

"For good reason, the early church fathers and the medieval scholastics regarded pride as the worst, most insidious of the seven deadly sins. Lanier Burns explains why—straightforwardly and with an eye to practicality that can disguise the profundity of his insight. The bad news is that pride infects us to the core of our depraved being; but the good news is that humility causes godliness to seep into all our thoughts and ways in counteractive redemption. Burns captures this dynamic and describes the sanctifying process in ways real and accessible. Of the many takeaways that this book offers, I probably most appreciated Burns's matter-of-fact investigations of Moses, Job, and Jesus, who each uniquely illustrate that although humility may not prevent hardship, it will take one through hardship with greater godliness of character and greater closeness with God on the other side. Not every book inculcates godliness of character into the reader who meditates on its thesis—but this is one such book."

—**R. Todd Mangum**, Clemens Professor of Missional Theology, Biblical Theological Seminary

"Lanier Burns has put us in his debt by producing a carefully researched and thoroughly biblical study. Years of teaching and theological reflection are evident throughout and enrich the work with depth and maturity. It is particularly gratifying to have a substantive study—not something trite and trivial—that puts the heel of its boot squarely on the neck of self-promotion and pride: a 'new virtue' that threatens our lives and churches. Read it and find 'the way of wise living, godly significance, and eternal meaning in a dying world.' I recommend it with fear and trembling."

—**Jay Smith**, Professor of New Testament Studies, Dallas Theological Seminary

PRIDE
AND
HUMILITY
AT WAR

PRIDE
AND
HUMILITY
AT WAR

A Biblical Perspective

J. LANIER BURNS

P&R
PUBLISHING
P.O. BOX 817 • PHILLIPSBURG • NEW JERSEY 08865-0817

To my students, who have encouraged me to write this book
on a most difficult subject,
especially the Brians, Bain and Bittiker,
who have taken the words and example of the Lord to heart

Contents

Contents

Foreword

IN HIS EARLY years as a maturing theologian, John Calvin encountered some striking words tucked away in a letter Augustine of Hippo had written in A.D. 410. They "delighted" the young reformer:

> When a certain rhetorician was asked what was the chief rule in eloquence, he replied, "Delivery"; what was the second rule, "Delivery"; what was the third rule, "Delivery"; so if you ask me concerning the precepts of the Christian religion, first, second, third, and always I would answer, "Humility."[1]

It might seem strange, therefore, that so little extensive study, writing, and perhaps teaching and preaching have focused on humility. Scholars might point to the older influence of Thomas

---

1. John Calvin, *Institutes of the Christian Religion*, 2 vols., ed. John T. McNeill, trans. Ford Lewis Battles, Library of Christian Classics, vol. 20 (Philadelphia: Westminster, 1960), 2.2.11. The reference is to Augustine's letter. Calvin had just turned thirty when he first embedded the quotation in earlier editions of his *Institutes*. The "certain rhetorician" is a reference to Demosthenes.

Aquinas, who specifically rejected the view that humility is a cardinal virtue and "reduced" its significance by treating it as a species of modesty, which he in turn saw as a subset of temperance.[2] But the real reason probably lies much closer to home. For who possesses the humility that would seem to be a prerequisite to teaching others about humility? Humility is also no more valued in the contemporary world than it was in the culture of the Roman Empire when it was first invaded by the gospel. Nor is this true only of the world. Indeed, one could be forgiven for wondering if at least parts of the evangelical church today fall foul of Luther's critique of the medieval church. They thirsted for a theology of glory (*theologia gloriae*) rather than a theology of the cross (*theologia crucis*)—seeking "influence" and "image" just as we have self-promoted through public and social media. Humility has hardly been front and center on the evangelical agenda.

Now, thankfully, Professor Lanier Burns has come to our help in this splendid biblical-theological and pastoral-theological study. He begins in the right place—by presenting himself not as one who has mastered his subject but as a fellow-learner, who sits beside us and follows with us on the biblical road map that provides the directions we need. He thus unconsciously illustrates the humility of mindset and approach that we need if we are to make progress in the Spirit. And while *Pride and Humility at War* is a patient biblical study, sensitive to the value of careful technical exegesis (as the footnotes make clear), it is written in a style that should appeal to every reader. As a result, Dr. Burns "allows" God's Word to speak for itself (if we may so speak) and to do its own work in us as we read it.

What C. S. Lewis once wisely wrote to an aspiring young author applies equally to aspiring teachers and preachers: we

2. In his *Summa Theologiae*, 2.2 Q.161.

should never tell our audience *how they ought to feel* about something, but rather describe that something in a manner that will
lead them to feel that way. It is all very well to be told that humility
is a key virtue or that we ought to be humble. But the question
is "How?" The contemporary Christian world has a tendency to
leave the question either unanswered ("Work out for yourself
how to do it") or artificially answered ("Here are the five things
you need to do"). But the sad truth is that anything we can do
is not likely to promote humility! We too easily forget the focus
of our Lord's prayer: "Sanctify them in the truth; your word is
truth" (John 17:17). When God's Word is patiently unfolded, it
both brings light and does its own work in us, transforming us
by the renewing of our minds (Rom. 12:1–2).

It is this approach—the Jesus and Paul Method, as it were—
that Dr. Burns employs so successfully, unfolding the teaching
of Scripture stage by stage from the patriarchs to the apostles.
In *Pride and Humility at War* he comes to us as a servant—not
only of the Word of God incarnate and in Scripture but also of
the people of God. In doing so he invites us to grow in grace with
him—growing downward into the presence of God so that we
will grow upward in likeness to Christ. This book is a love gift
to the church and breathes the spirit of an author who comes to
us saying, "The Lord Jesus has given me this to share with you."
May the "loaves and fishes" he brings here be blessed, broken,
and multiplied in our lives!

Sinclair B. Ferguson
Chancellor's Professor of Systematic Theology
Reformed Theological Seminary

Acknowledgments

TO MY FRIENDS at P&R Publishing, who have allowed me to take the time and freedom to ponder things that have stretched me to the limit.

To Collin Huber, who generously helped to prepare the manuscript for publication.

And to my beloved wife of fifty years, who read the manuscript and insisted that humility is important and must be applied to our daily struggles and challenges.

Abbreviations

BECNT	Baker Exegetical Commentary on the New Testament
EBC	Expositor's Bible Commentary
ESV	English Standard Version
ICC	International Critical Commentary
JETS	*Journal of the Evangelical Theological Society*
LCL	Loeb Classical Library
LXX	Septuagint
NICOT	New International Commentary on the Old Testament (Grand Rapids: Eerdmans, 1976–93)
NIDNTT	*New International Dictionary of New Testament Theology*, 4 vols., ed. Colin Brown (Grand Rapids: Zondervan, 1976)
NIV	New International Version

OTL	Old Testament Library
SNTSMS	Society for New Testament Studies Monograph Series (Cambridge, MA: Cambridge University Press)
TDNT	Gerhard Kittel and Gerhard Friedrich, eds., *Theological Dictionary of the New Testament*, 10th ed. (Grand Rapids: Eerdmans, 1984)
TOTC	Tyndale Old Testament Commentaries (London: Inter-Varsity Press, 1973–74)
WBC	Word Biblical Commentary
WSC	Westminster Shorter Catechism

1

Introduction

CONSCIENTIOUS CHRISTIANS ARE in daily battles with easily besetting temptations, misplaced priorities, alluring compromises, and broken relationships in a world that weakens them with its complexities, options, stresses, and seductive values. A student recently told me that pride had caused him endless frustration and anxiety. He was afraid that he would not be able to find a place of significance in this life, that he would disappoint the expectations of his family—a fear that he would have to cheat to get ahead. These struggles to understand and achieve some victory over vices are as old as history, and we seem to be as far as ever from answers and relief. They are formative elements of our identity and sourced from our heart, the center of our ambitions and decisions. What are the sources and causes of these struggles in our midst? Why do we achieve our goals with a nagging sense of disappointment after discovering that it was not what it seemed when we started? The consensus of the Bible and the history of Christian doctrine points to a perennial cause at the center of human life: the conflict between pride and humility. C. S. Lewis referred to these opposites as "that part of Christian morals where they differ most sharply from all other morals. . . . The vice I am talking of is Pride or Self-Conceit: and the virtue opposite to it, in Christian morals, is called Humility."[1]

The virtues in general and humility in particular have fallen on hard times in the modern world. Even people who try to follow Christ are uneasy about humility, though they know that God promised blessing for the humble. It seems so weak in a world that honors power and bravado. Pop psychology has identified humility as an enemy of self-esteem; oppressed minorities feel that it is a ploy to dismantle their bid for entitlements; some philosophers and theologians have tried to affirm a "will to power" as the only way that will succeed in the world. Everywhere we turn, we compare ourselves with others around us. Competitiveness has been built into all of the institutions in the modern world. The focus has shifted from families to corporations, and modern social sciences quantify success and significance by status and rank. Competitive ranking begins with grades in grammar school. The military ranks with stripes and ribbons. The business world uses titles, salaries, bonuses, and office space to signify value and worth. The issue is performance in a hierarchy of power. Small wonder that modernity has exposed disappointments, depression, and even suicide, since marketing is geared to a small circle of elites and winners. All of my life I have been taught that "man's chief end is to glorify God and to enjoy him forever" (true humility). But all of my life I have observed that we live for greater profits and our own pleasure until we die (true pride). According to the Bible, the church is a family where artificial distinctions are melted by God's grace and a common bond in Jesus Christ, hence "there is neither Jew nor Greek, there is neither slave nor free, there is neither male

---

1. C. S. Lewis, *Mere Christianity* (1952; repr., San Francisco: HarperSanFrancisco, 2001), 121.

nor female" (Gal. 3:28). The world has persuaded us that pride is natural—to the point that we think of ourselves in terms of our superiority over others, and our agenda is to control them to our advantage. Without careful thought humility seems so often unrealistic, impractical, or demeaning—really not a virtue for this time and place.

My interest in this subject began a number of years ago, when I encountered stunning statements that contradicted the obvious ways of the world. First of these was "the last will be first." I did not know of a single champion or hero who thought this way in any field: athletics, business, politics, education, science, or any other professional commitment. Self-interest, we are told, is the engine that runs the world. It is an undeniable motivator as evidenced by the single-minded devotion of people who train sacrificially every day to be the mythical "best" in their passion or expertise. The problem with the improbable promise of "winning by losing" is that it was made by Jesus Christ, meaning that sincere Christians must come to terms with it.

Second, I encountered comprehensive statements by noteworthy Christians that, if correct, demanded careful reflection. Their weightiness challenged common views of Christianity. For example, Andrew Murray wrote, "Humility, the place of entire dependence on God, is, from the very nature of things, the first duty and the highest virtue of man. It is the root of every virtue. And so pride, or the loss of this humility, is the root of every sin and evil."[2] Is humility not one of many virtues? How do we demonstrate that it is the root of every virtue? Similarly, Jon Bloom has written about the opposing vice of pride. "Pride turns ambition selfish, perverts sexual desire into unspeakable lusts, interprets net worth as self-worth, infects the wound of grief and loss with the bacteria of bitterness, and twists competition

2. Andrew Murray, *Humility* (New Kensington, PA: Whitaker House, 1982), 16.

into conquest."[3] Is this not confusing pride with a panoply of evils? What is this vice that robs life of joy?

Third, fifty years in ministry have taught me that humble servants of Christ have enjoyed remarkable significance in the Lord's family. Of course, biblical examples, especially our Lord, are oft cited and well known. "One Solitary Life" poetically celebrates our Savior, who "did none of the things usually associated with greatness," nevertheless, he "is the central figure of the human race" and affected life on earth more than all armies, parliaments, and kings.[4] But was the Lord great by worldly standards? Was he not "solitary" and crucified? We can observe that Christian service has been distinguished by people whose "small" ministries to the hungry, abandoned, and sickly will be commended by the King. "Truly, I say to you, as you did it to one of the least of these my brothers, you did it to me" (Matt. 25:40). I am sure that many of these are people that I have known in business, on mission fields, or in churches—anywhere a deep and lasting impact has been made in God's family by loving brothers and sisters. Probably we have all seen authentic humility in people we most admire.

How do we define humility and pride so that we can align our lives with biblical priorities? The Greeks and Hellenists, who profoundly influenced Western traditions, thought of humility as lowly, insignificant, weak, poor, or servile. In their culture humility was excessively base, deficient, and without pleasure. It was almost always used when speaking disparagingly of people or cities, who usually used obsequious behavior to curry favors. Aristotle (ca. 300 B.C.) in his *Nicomachean Ethics* argued that humility hindered the development of virtue. Humiliated people

3. Jon Bloom, "Don't Let Pride Steal Your Joy!," *Revive* 46, 2 (2015): 14.

4. A number of versions of "One Solitary Life" have been adapted from James Allan Francis's sermon "The Real Jesus," in *The Real Jesus and Other Sermons* (Philadelphia: Judson, 1926).

and cities displayed their weakness and lack of virtue by their condition, which was epitomized by slavery.

The highest aim of humanity was happiness, which differed among "the wise" (privileged) and the "majority" (unprivileged). The common good of happiness was to be pursued over one's lifetime through the active exercise of the soul in conformity with the virtues. So the right activity reflected a moderate pride that held one's head high in all circumstances; a willful self-sufficiency; and a stable disposition among family, friends, and city. However, excessive pride was an overweening vice in which one sought inappropriate (or excessive) honor and acclaim.[5]

In the aristocratic culture of ancient Greece, the worth of men was determined by parentage, and a virtue (ἀρετή) was an inherited ability that enabled them to function well in society: civically, militarily, and morally. It was reflected in excellence of performance and nobility of character. This is illustrated in virtues like *magnificence*, which mandated large contributions from abundant wealth, and *magnanimity*, in which the great-souled acknowledged the lofty honor that came with their possession of all the virtues. They could be truthful about their greatness and unconcerned about the excesses of boastfulness or self-depreciation. The notion of divine standards of human morality, the foundation of biblical ethics, was absent for the Greeks. The society of gods merely replicated human drives and behaviors.[6]

Though some like Socrates held that virtues could be taught,

---

5. "Unlike the ὑβριστής, who acts violently in spite of divine and human law, and the ἀλαζών, the empty boaster who deceives himself and others by making the most of his advantages, abilities and achievements, the ὑπερήφανος is the one who with pride, arrogance and foolish presumption brags of his position, power and wealth and despises others." *TDNT*, s.v. "ὑπερήφανος," by Georg Bertram, 8.525. This is the excess beyond the moderate mean. Plato contrasts honorable, respectable citizens with the arrogant, who are puffed up and annoying.

6. See Robert Payne, *The Wanton Nymph: A Study of Pride* (London: Heinemann, 1951).

nothing changed their pervasively negative view of humility. The possibility of teaching virtue was predicated on a distinction between intellectual virtues (teachable) and moral virtues (innate character). Epictetus distinctively taught that there is a common humanity that merits friendly relationships, but humility for him remained negative as a petty, inferior disposition.[7] Then ταπεινός was rarely used to mean obedience; it referred to adaptation to one's place in state, army, and family to maintain order. It involved a pride in status, not abasement—a necessary means to avoid the chaos of extreme behaviors by the underprivileged. Absent was any suggestion of the last becoming first.

Theologians in the Middle Ages generally attempted to balance biblical teaching with the views of Hellenism. Christianity had at least three traditions with a bearing on our understanding of humility and pride. First, Pelagius (ca. A.D. 400) rejected original sin (Augustinian depravity) and affirmed that people had been created with an ability to live sinlessly, a condition that continued after the fall. He could not accept human frailty as an excuse for the immorality that he observed. God may assist virtuous living, but people were blameworthy for choosing pride (or arrogance) when they didn't have to.

Second, Augustine (ca. A.D. 400) opposed Pelagius by teaching human depravity and the inability of people to live virtuously apart from the grace of God. His *Confessions* (A.D. 378) frequently contrasts pride and humility.[8] Pride was the character trait of the unconverted, and humility was the foundational virtue of the church. Augustine defined pride as the creature's refusal to submit to God, that is, as rebellion. He held that God ordered his creation so that one could not escape his sovereign presence. Thus, evil angels and people were caught in a self-destructive vortex, in which they turned inward to find purpose and feed on

---

7. Dissertationes, 3.24.
8. See also *De trinitate* (ca. A.D. 415) and *De civitate Dei* (ca. A.D. 425).

themselves in search of satisfaction. Only a humble believer, he held, could follow Christ. Humility was not in the first instance an attitude toward oneself, but rather a willingness to let God be supreme, with consequent love for other people. In other words, humility meant dependence on God's enablement, gratitude for his gracious blessings, acceptance of Christ's example as the only normative guide in this life, and faithful practice of contrition for one's sins.

Third, Thomas Aquinas (ca. A.D. 1240) is known for his attempt to synthesize Aristotelian philosophy ("the Philosopher" in the *Summa*) and Christian principles. He discussed humility in depth in his *Summa Theologica Secunda Secundae*, Q. 161. He frequently agrees with Augustine and cites him in conjunction with a number of other early Fathers. As a theological virtue (versus civic ability), humility is the foundation of Christian spirituality. As the opposite of pride, it is based on worshipful subjection to God and "comprehends the whole of Christian teaching," notably Christ's humility in providing salvation. Reverence for God should lead to one's subjection to all neighbors for his sake. Humility is also the inward moderation and restraint of passions and appetites (under the broader heading of temperance).[9]

Fourth, a number of theologians developed depravity on a trajectory of the worthlessness of the sinner, which affected perceptions of humility in a very negative way. Benedict of Nursia (ca. A.D. 540) founded Western monasticism and formulated his Rule to promote the abdication of self-will to fight for "our true King." The steps to truth are humility, compassion, and contemplation. Benedict defined humility as "a virtue by which man acquires a low view of himself because he knows himself

---

9. In Roman Catholic tradition the cardinal virtues are prudence, justice, fortitude, and temperance. Humility is annexed to temperance, which is primary in the restraint of inordinate desires.

well." His practices included twelve degrees of humility, the first of which was "always having the fear of God before one's eyes" as evidenced in strict obedience. The seventh degree was "not only with his tongue but also in his inmost soul believeth, that he is the lowest and vilest of men . . . saying with the Prophet, 'But I am a worm and no man, the reproach of men and the outcast of the people.'"[10] The degrees, as we would expect, were to be understood in terms of monastic life. The first six involve contempt for fellow monastics; the next four contempt for one's superiors; and the last two contempt for God. For Benedict, contempt is synonymous with pride.

Anselm of Canterbury (ca. A.D. 1100) lived most of his adult life in the Benedictine order. Like Benedict, he thought of humility as a staged progression, only with seven levels instead of Benedict's twelve. These are recorded in his *De Similitudinibus* and *De Anselm* (esp. chap. 1). His progression was from the valley of pride, which was "the depth of human vice," up the "mountain of humility," which was necessary for the attainment of other moral virtues. The prize at the summit was virtuous self-knowledge. The vices reflected ignorance of one's unworthiness. The levels of humility proceed from the acknowledgment that one is contemptible up to "loving contemptible treatment from others."[11]

One problem among many is that this view of self-hatred is not humility as presented by the Bible and biblically oriented Christian traditions. If humility is contrition over our sinful condition, then Jesus could hardly have been its exemplar. In spite of sin, "God so loved the world" (John 3:16) that he humbled

---

10. Benedict, *Rule*, rev. ed., trans. Boniface Verheyen (Atchison, KS: St. Benedict's Abbey, 1949), chap. 7, first and seventh degree.

11. A further example of worm theology is Walter Hilton's *The Stairway of Perfection*, trans. M. L. Del Mastro (Garden City, NY: Doubleday, 1979), 80–81: "First of all, this is how you must practice humility. You must be unable to dwell among men and unworthy to serve God in conversation with his servants. . . . You shall judge yourself more foul and more wretched than any creature alive." Hilton was a fourteenth-century mystic.

himself to save it. Ironically, the notion of self-hatred encourages attitudes and activities that easily gravitate toward pride: a "superior" inferior view of oneself in comparison with fellow believers.

Fifth, Martin Luther expressed Augustinian depravity as *in se curvatos* and represents the views of major Reformers. After the fall the human spirit "curved in on itself" for vain self-glorification and pride. In his words,

> It is easy to understand how in these things we seek our fulfillment and love ourselves, how we are turned in upon ourselves and become in grown at least in our heart, even when we cannot sense it in our actions . . . our nature has been so deeply curved in upon itself because of the viciousness of original sin . . . nor can he be freed of his perversity . . . except by the grace of God.[12]

Noteworthy here is the inward curve of the original sin of pride, which could only be healed by the grace of God.

The Western view of the human condition took a radical turn away from Christian traditions to the European Enlightenment. Scientific research and naturalistic philosophy were enlarged into intellectual forces. The Catholic Church aided the changes with censorial responses to views that challenged its authority. This change to modernity (ca. seventeenth century to the present) has been insightfully described by Robert Solomon:

> In much of Western tradition, the central demand of modern philosophy is *the autonomy of the individual person*. This means that each of us must be credited with the ability to ascertain what is true and what is right, through our own thinking and

---

12. Martin Luther, *Luther's Works*, ed. Hilton Oswald (St. Louis: Concordia, 1972), 25.245, 291, 313.

experience, without depending upon outside authority: parents, teachers, popes, kings, or a majority of peers. . . . What it means is that whether you believe in God or not, for example, must be decided by you, by appeal to your own reason and arguments that you can formulate and examine by yourself. . . . This stress on individual *autonomy* stands at the very foundation of contemporary Western thought. We might say that it is our most basic assumption.[13]

Solomon's summarizing statement profoundly describes contemporary thought and the intellectual move from ecclesial tradition to secular individualism. This, in turn, effected a change in how pride and humility came to be viewed. Pride became a virtue, and humility became a vice. The world of traditional values was turned upside down.

Friedrich Nietzsche best illustrates this exaltation of pride (1844–1900). He wanted to revive classical ethics and remove the self-deceptions of the church. He stated that humility had really been a strategic device to topple people who were dominant and powerful in society. It was a slave morality that promoted lowliness and weakness to make the naturally virtuous attainment of power and flagrant self-approval appear flawed. In reality one doesn't win by losing. For Nietzsche, humility is despicable because it hypocritically seeks to exalt itself by pointing to the guilt of the privileged. The "natural attitude" is pride as arrogant self-promotion to attain as much personal power as possible.[14]

Nietzsche represents the philosophical shift, but other writers illustrate how deeply the transformation affected the cultural

13. Robert C. Solomon, *Introducing Philosophy: A Text with Integrated Readings*, 9th ed. (New York: Oxford University Press, 2008), 16–17.

14. Friedrich Nietzsche, *The Will to Power*, trans Walter Kaufmann and R. J. Hollingdale, ed. Walter Kaufmann (New York: Vintage, 1968). See also Robert Solomon, ed., *Nietzsche: A Collection of Critical Essays* (Notre Dame, IN: University of Notre Dame, 1973), especially chapter 8 by Philippa Foot, "Nietzsche: The Revaluation of Values."

milieu. Ayn Rand, for example, used the lengthy speech of the god-like John Galt to explain her "Objectivist Philosophy":

> The real world is not the product of your sins, it is the product and the image of your virtues.... Pride is the recognition of the fact that you are your own highest value, and, like all of man's values, it has to be earned—that of any achievements open to you, the one that makes all others possible is the creation of your own character—that your character, your actions, your desires, your emotions are the products of the premises held by your mind—that ... he must acquire the values of character that make his life worth sustaining—that as man is a being of self-made wealth, so he is a being of self-made soul—that to live requires a sense of self-value, but man, who has no automatic values, has no automatic sense of self-esteem and must earn it by shaping his soul in the image of his moral ideal, in the image of Man, the rational being he is born able to create, but must create by choice—that the first precondition of self-esteem is that radiant selfishness of soul which desires the best in all things ... a soul that seeks above all else to achieve its own moral perfection.[15]

Rand underscored the virtues of autonomy and pride (self-sufficiency and self-centeredness) in creating the modern world of virtue. She denied God and grace: "you are your own highest value" and "you have to earn it." We must create not only our resources but also our character. The moral ideal, turning the *imago Dei* into unreality, is Man, who must be generated from a "radiant

15. Ayn Rand, *Atlas Shrugged* (New York: Signet, 1957), 936, 946–47. Rand continued to quote her Galt speech in explaining her position. In a University of Wisconsin Symposium on "Ethics in Our Time" she delivered a paper entitled "The Objectivist Ethics," in *The Virtue of Selfishness: A New Concept of Egoism* (New York: Signet, 1964), 27: "To live for his own sake means that *the achievement of his own happiness is man's highest moral purpose.*"

selfishness." This is an explicit denial of biblical and traditional values; in this cruel world may the best and fittest survive.

A similar but less caustic presentation of the same emphasis was made in Robert Ringer's best-selling *Looking Out for #1*. He cited Aristotle's goal of happiness as a universal priority and agreed with "John Galt's" philosophy.[16] His admonition was "to forget foundationless tradition, forget the 'moral' standards others may have tried to cram down your throat, forget the beliefs people may have tried to intimidate you into accepting as 'right.'"[17] His dedication to Number One is important "because it leads to a simple, uncomplicated life in which you spend more time doing those things which give you the greatest amount of pleasure," which is "to feel good."[18] Always remember, he emphasized, "that happiness is that which makes you feel good."[19] To do this a person must win as often as possible by whatever means. His nemesis is "the Absolute Moralist, the creature who spends his life deciding what is right for you. . . . If he believes in Christ, he's certain that it's his moral duty to help you 'see the light.'"[20] Reality is, and no one should speculate about what it ought to be. "No other living person has the right to decide what is moral (right or wrong) for you."[21] Ringer advocates absolute autonomy and no accountability before God: there is no right way to live. So he summarily dismisses humility as an accurate assessment of oneself and canonizes pride with Self as "Number One." Ringer brings us full circle from classical philosophers without apparent awareness of their objection to obnoxious arrogance and the absence of a sense of civic responsibility. He dismisses

16. Robert J. Ringer, *Looking Out for Number #1* (New York: Fawcett Crest, 1977), 14. Ringer also wrote *Winning through Intimidation*.

17. Ringer, *Looking Out for Number #1*, 8.

18. Ibid., 12.

19. Ibid., 17.

20. Ibid., 20.

21. Ibid.

the cautionary tales of ecclesial traditions about the need for humility in community and the destructiveness of pride. In other words, how can life bring pleasure if your Number One is at war with everyone else's Number One? If history has demonstrated anything, it has shown that sinners have agreed about very little except that we do not want God to govern our lives or the world. Ringer joins Rand and Nietzsche in a naïve assumption that liberated people in a valueless world will address the deep needs of humanity such as salvation, justice, peace, and joy, which have been elusive to this point.

We have journeyed from ancient to modern times attempting to define humility and pride. We have seen that each generation gravitates to meanings in accordance with their social and cultural contexts. A bewildering array of meanings has resulted in a confusing kaleidoscope of nuances. Can we use *humility* and *pride* in a coherent way that will enhance mutual understanding of their contrast?

We close this discussion with definitions from an English dictionary.[22] *Virtue* is defined as moral excellence and righteousness, such as patience; an effective or beneficial quality; an advantage; an effective force or power; and ability to produce a definite result. Note that virtue is a purely human trait with not even an inference that God is relevant. No mention is made about whether a virtue is innate or acquired, though we could assume that the definition would include both. A virtuous person is righteous, effective, and skilled—"successful" perhaps captures the sense. *Humility* is meekness or modesty in behavior, attitude, or spirit; low in rank or quality; degradation. The verbal forms mean to lower in pride, dignity, or self-respect; to disgrace. We should note that the meanings range from a neutral modesty to a negative

22. For this purpose we have used *The American Heritage® College Writer's Dictionary* (Boston: Houghton Mifflin Harcourt, 2013), hoping that this kind of dictionary may come closest to public parlance.

degradation with loss of dignity or self-respect. The weight of the equivocation is in the direction of negative and undesirable. *Pride* is a sense of one's proper dignity and self-respect; pleasure or satisfaction taken in an achievement or association; a source of pleasure or satisfaction; the best of a group; and an excessively high opinion of oneself or conceit. We note that, as with humility, different meanings are assigned to the same concept. It seems that the ambiguity of historical uses of the contrast has found its way into the dictionary. When does proper dignity slide into conceit in a modern setting where the shift has been explicitly made? The definitions seem to agree with classical emphases on one's proper place in social orders without obnoxious braggadocio. A modern meaning enters when pleasure and satisfaction come from being the best of a group.

We cannot examine in detail concepts that range from denigration to exaltation, from humanistic virtues to God-oriented enablement, from an ability not to sin to innately proud, from self-hatred to self-worship, and also include the pivotal reversal of humility/pride as virtue/vice and vice/virtue respectively. What is a realistic goal for this study? The history of interpretation has surfaced a number of questions that are worthy of extended discussion. However, the greater need is a thorough analysis of how the Bible uses pride and humility. This is our goal. Hopefully, this analysis will serve as a center to orient the incredible diversity of views and the centrality of God to any discussion of the subject. Our discussion of the Bible will begin with the Pentateuch and progressively trace the contrast through blocks of Scripture, culminating in the New Testament Epistles. Chapters on the Wisdom Literature and the Prophets will lay the foundation for the difficult discussion of the contrast between pride and humility in the Gospels. Jesus Christ was the primary expositor and exemplar of a godly understanding of humility, and we would do well to embrace him as our guide on this pilgrimage.

Summary

We have surveyed various views of humility and pride through history to show their different meanings, from denigration to conceit. From the beginnings of human history, virtues and vices have had social connotations that promote community or divisions and war. Even without explicit biblical emphases, God (or the gods) emerge as vital for any discussion. In the Bible God is the standard by which humility and pride are defined and discerned. Indeed, they can be important entry points for thinking about the notion of covenant in God's relationship with his people. Humility is submissive dependence on the Lord on his terms, while pride is rebellion against God's covenantal guidelines.

Key Terms

automatic. In anthropology, an innate or intuitive response to circumstances.

autonomy. The assumption that an individual is free to make judgments and decisions apart from outside authorities (such as God).

bravado. Boastfulness or bragging about one's accomplishments or character.

censorial. Judgmental assessment of content that is objectionable to moral standards, usually involving punishment.

criterion. A standard by which a judgment is made.

ecclesial. Pertaining to church matters.

Enlightenment. The European movement in the seventeenth and eighteenth centuries that emphasized reason and autonomy rather than tradition and revelation.

heart. In the Bible this stands for the center of the person and the matrix for thinking about our place in family and society.

The equivalent today is the brain as biological center of the person.

Hellenism. The culture of ancient Greece.

intuitive. Instinctive acceptance of truth without conscious reasoning.

mythical. Concepts or ideas that are characteristic of cultures, often concerning idealized values.

natural philosophy. The belief that only natural laws and forces operate in the world as opposed to transcendent or supernatural forces such as God.

significance. Worthy of attention, social importance.

vice. A human practice or habit that characterizes evil, degrading, or immoral behavior.

virtue. A human practice or habit that characterizes moral excellence or a beneficial character trait.

Questions for Discussion

1. When we speak of humility and pride as the sources of righteousness and evil respectively, what does the metaphor of a "root" mean?
2. Why is personal worth always tied to wealth throughout history?
3. Humility was regarded as servile in ancient cultures. Why was "servant" a title of honor in the New Testament (Rom. 1:1; James 1:1)?
4. Is our goal in life "to glorify God, and to enjoy him for ever"?[23]
5. What was Augustine's view of humility and pride, and why is his view suitable as a prelude for the rest of the book?
6. How can self-denigration, so-called worm theology, lead to pride?

23. WSC Q.1.

7. How does Ringer's modern preference for pride differ from the views of classical philosophers?

For Further Reading

Lewis, C. S. *Mere Christianity*. 1952. Reprint, San Francisco: HarperSanFrancisco, 2001. Chapter 8 is one of the best introductory presentations on pride and humility.

Ramm, Bernard L. *Offense to Reason: A Theology of Sin*. San Francisco: Harper & Row, 1985. Ramm condenses a broad survey of the subject into a few readable chapters. The middle of the book, the center and "root" of sin, is particularly noteworthy.

2

God-Centeredness or Self-Centeredness in the Pentateuch

RON STARED AT his computer as he recalled the death of his family's dreams over the last year. He and Betty *had* seen an opportunity to upgrade their home for their growing family. They had found a wonderful house that was convenient for their educational, social, and business needs. But it was large and expensive!

They contacted a real estate agent, who assured them that they could afford the move by combining their hard-earned savings with easy money from mortgage lenders, who offer subprime loans for higher interest rates. Ron and Betty felt anxious about the doubled mortgage payments, which would extend into their retirement years. But the agent assured them that the money would be insured by "mortgage-backed securities," making it an investment rather than a debt. They sensed this was virtual reality without a solid financial basis, but they persuaded themselves that they needed the house.

Could they have foreseen that a simple desire to own a better home would be part and parcel of a national scam with world-wide implications? Could they have anticipated that a hope-filled bubble would burst, leaving them without a home and possibly without a job? Many fellow workers at Ron's office had shared the unlimited possibilities of the economy. His dream house had been foreclosed, so Ron surfed the Internet to see what people in similar situations were doing. One discouraging blog from Steve caught his attention:

> Greed has always been with us. It has an unlimited number of guises. In this case mortgage lenders took bad loans to make more money at the expense of the public. When the dot.com bubble burst, it was greed by venture capitalists, Wall Street, and investors driving up the prices on speculation. Greed has so many guises that there can be no guarantee that something like this will not happen again. People love money and are never satisfied with enough, so it's bound to happen again.

As Ron pondered his family's fall, he angrily wondered how wealthy, powerful people could hurt the country and ordinary citizens. How could executives and politicians be rewarded with exorbitant bonuses when he and Betty had lost everything in the deceitfulness of the social system around them? Why did God let this happen, and how would Pastor Stephens explain their dilemma?

We will examine Ron's questions in light of biblical theology. The reversal of his and Betty's fortune involves some of the Bible's most important insights about human nature. We prefer not to think about a fall from paradise as an explanation for the evil and human vices in the world, because it casts a negative shadow over our character and relationships. We prefer to think optimistically: that we are basically good people, and that with hard work and high ambitions we can save ourselves from our chain of dilemmas. We prefer this approach until we fall like Ron and Betty. Then we realize that the world has suffered a cataclysmic reversal in the past that explains not only the sinful state of the world but also God's answer to our problems in Jesus Christ. Greed is one of a cluster of vices that the Scriptures identify as self-centeredness, which has been comprehensively labeled pride. We will think about the beginning and spread of sin under four headings:

1. The Human Condition from Adam through Abraham
2. Moses as an Example of Humility in Israel
3. Moses' Prediction of Pride in Israel
4. The Foundational Conflict between God and Self

Genesis explains humanity's sin as our refusal to accept God's limitations as creatures. We rebel against God and harm other people for our selfish advantage. The gracious presence of the Holy Spirit transforms pride into humility, a change that enables us to joyfully serve God and to experience his blessing. We will use Moses to illustrate that humble servants of the LORD have a personal relationship with God that seems strange to the self-seeking world around them. Finally, in Deuteronomy 8, Moses predicted that the Israelites would become prosperous, and because of pride they would cease to observe the Word and walk in the Lord's ways. By God's grace, we will humbly seek to understand ourselves better in the light of his Word, lest we lose face with people like Ron and Betty as we compete for our interests in the world.

The Human Condition from Adam through Abraham

The incipient beginning of humility's antithesis to pride is rooted in God's creation of humanity in his image (Gen. 1:26–28).

The passage is filled with interpretive issues. Most germane to our topic is God's forming Adam and Eve for covenantal relationship with himself and ordaining that they would rule the world under his sovereignty. The verb for creation (*bara'*) is used three times in verse 27, leaving no doubt that the high point and goal of God's creative genius was humanity. Their authoritative dominion over God's earthly order meant that they were active, purposeful creatures rather than passive observers in a fatalistic world.[1]

The aggressiveness of mankind is supported by several details. They were to reproduce "living creatures" to sustain their God-given dominion through history's generations (2:7, 20–25). They were to work in Eden to produce their nourishment (v. 15). And Adam named subordinate creatures to order life in the garden (vv. 1–20).[2] Humanity's purposeful dominion is foundational for pride and humility, for they are the antithetical responses to God's will for life on earth.

God directed the couple to abstain from the tree of the knowledge of good and evil, so that they would not experientially know evil and death (Gen. 2:17). Disobedience would separate the couple from the covenantal blessing of life with God and initiate decay in their bodies. As sinners they would be corrupt in their thoughts and practices apart from God's intervening grace. Accordingly, they would introduce certain death into creation, for their perverted rule would cause its decay as well. From the beginning, obedience to God's Word was the mark of humanity's dependence on God for life and successful rule.

---

1. Psalm 8 is David's reflection on creation, with an emphasis on humanity's rule under God: "You have given him dominion over the works of your hands; you have put all things under his feet" (v. 6).

2. The verb *radah* (1:26, 28) is different from the word meaning "dominion" in verse 16. *Radah* is paired with *kabash*, meaning "subdue," suggesting an active subjugation of lesser creatures.

Pride as Self-Centeredness

Satan's initial temptation craftily juxtaposed the couple's innate ambition to rule and God's goodness in his stipulation of obedience (Rev. 12:9; 20:2). Instead of focusing on their freedom to enjoy all but one of the trees, the venomous tempter emphasized the forbidden tree, thereby questioning the goodness of God. The woman responded by expanding God's command to include not touching the fruit, which set her up for a fall. Examining it without ill effect, she was ready for the tempter's outright denial of death for disobedience.

The lie paved the way for an insidious temptation that the couple could be more than creatures: "You will be like God, knowing good and evil" (Gen. 3:5).[3] Their unique capacities in the image and likeness of God had made them God-like but not divine. Thus, the issue involved not only the consequence of disobedience but also the false promise of attaining divine wisdom, which could rule without creaturely limitation. Behind the term rendered "a delight to the eyes" (ta'awah) was an intense desire that gave the temptation its force. The presumption to be God is the innermost core of sin, a pride that has malignantly short-circuited the Creator's blessings throughout history.[4] Camouflaged by the deceitful desirability of the fruit (v. 6), this sin led to their catastrophic fall and the corruption of every aspect of creation.

3. Jewish *midrash* viewed Adam's sleep during the creation of Eve as a mark of his creatureliness (*Midrash Rabbah*, Genesis 8, 4–5). God in rest celebrated his divine work of creation; Adam in rest celebrated God's creation of Eve. This check on self-deification was perpetuated in Sabbath observance, which was to be a worshipful rest as creatures under God.

4. Modern interpretations of the fall have tended to erode the sharp biblical distinction between Creator and creature by viewing sin with a relational emphasis on injustice and violence. For example, Marjorie Suchocki has defined sin as "participation through intent or act in unnecessary violence that contributes to the ill-being of any aspect of earth or its inhabitants." Suchocki, *The Fall to Violence* (New York: Continuum,

Disobedience, seemingly insignificant compared with capital offenses, actually meant that sin must be understood as a crime against God on what was once a "very good" earth. Without God as the object, there would be an incredible disproportion between the seriousness of the offense and the magnitude of the result. The foundation of potential sin was that a person was God's creature and was made to live in worshipful obedience under his Maker. Thus, sin is a revolt against creation's Sovereign in the circumstances of life. We must not forget that human authority was given only to uphold and enforce God's ultimate sovereignty, not as an independent gift in any sense. Disobedience is pride or self-centeredness, which means that obedient submission is biblical humility. We must understand from this point forward that without a biblical understanding of God, there is no meaningful concept of sin—only inexplicable evil or man's inhumanity to man. Nor is there a meaningful concept of humility, which has been reduced to a vacuous ideal in a violent world. When the first couple stepped out from the simplicity of obedience to God, possessing forbidden knowledge, they initiated an absurd movement, which has ever since imagined that people could do whatever they wanted apart from God without life-threatening consequences.

In theological terms the corruption of creation through humanity's rebellion against the Creator resulted in "total depravity." In his *Institutes of the Christian Religion*, John Calvin affirmed that God "inveighs not against particular men but against the whole race of Adam's children."[5] Sin, he held, is a

1995), 12. Though injustice and violence were consequences of the fall, in this view sin would involve God as he and the world mutually experience one another.

5. John Calvin, *Institutes of the Christian Religion*, 2 vols., ed. John T. McNeill, trans. Ford Lewis Battles, et al., Library of Christian Classics, vol. 20 (Philadelphia: Westminster, 1960), 2.3.2. Earlier Calvin had attributed evil to "depravity of nature" or "the corruption of nature" (ibid., 1.14.3). This emphasis has a wider circulation than most people realize. We may note Aviad Kleinberg: "All sins are reruns of the original

human condition that affects the whole person and not merely a particular aspect such as will or reason. The fall infected all people "with ambition and pride, together with ungratefulness because Adam by seeking more than was granted him shamefully spurned God's great bounty, which had been lavished upon him."[6] Pride became innate "so that there is, indeed, nothing that man's nature seeks more eagerly than to be flattered."[7] This self-delusion of grandeur led to death, because the memory of scandalized nobility generated a downward spiral of obstinate disobedience attempting to recapture the loss.

The fall introduced a continuity of depravity in "original sin." As representative of all humanity, Adam "consigned his race to ruin by his rebellion when he perverted the whole order of nature in heaven and on earth."[8] Therefore, Calvin concluded, "all of us, who have descended from impure seed, are born infected with the contagion of sin. In fact, before we saw the light of this life, we were soiled and spotted in God's sight."[9] Sin has infected every person with a miserable servitude to sin. The human condition was rendered hopeless apart from the gracious intervention of God on behalf of his people.

The biblical account of the fall seems harsh to many people,

---

sin, the original pride. Each of our desires participates in the sin of pride, for the 'I' precedes desire, motivates it, and feeds it." 7 Deadly Sins: A Very Partial List (Cambridge: Harvard University Press, 2008), 138. Cf. Kaliprasada Sinha, The Self in Indian Philosophy (Calcutta: Punthi Pustak, 1991), which speaks of the self as an illusion that promotes passions that cause suffering. Thus, the Buddhist should seek to eradicate atman (the self). The Bible seeks to ground the self in the image of God, rather than the impossible goal of eradication.

6. Calvin, Institutes, 2.1.4.

7. Ibid.

8. Ibid., 2.1.5. Jack Collins cogently observes that creation is only the "arena of pain" under human perversion rather than "fallen" in its natural elements. Genesis 1–4: A Linguistic, Literary, and Theological Commentary (Phillipsburg, NJ: P&R Publishing, 2006), 164. "This is due not to a change in the properties of the ground but to the change in humanity and to God's providential purposes of chastisement" (ibid., 178).

9. Calvin, Institutes, 2.1.5.

who want to see themselves and their world in a positive light. But history and experience lead us to an encounter with the world as it is rather than to our preferred illusory fantasies. Of course, depravity encompasses genocidal dictators, gang leaders, contemporary corruptions, drug dealers, and related criminal behaviors. But are good people depraved? According to the Bible we are equally sinners, even if we are not equally depraved. We should be grateful for human kindnesses and generosity that enrich life on earth. However, in varying degrees, depravity embraces even good people, who also need the saving grace of God. Psalm 14:2–3 has no exceptions:

> The LORD looks down from heaven on the children of man,
>   to see if there are any who understand,
>   who seek after God.
> They have all turned aside; together they have become
>   corrupt;
>   there is none who does good,
>   not even one. (cf. Eccl. 7:20, 29)

Romans 3:22–23 emphasizes the same point, "For there is no distinction: for all have sinned and fall short of the glory of God." Marguerite Shuster captures the biblical emphasis, "Moved by pride and self-centeredness, we assert ourselves over against the authority of God our Maker, and over against the rights and claims of our neighbor."[10]

Interestingly, Jesus condemned the scribes and Pharisees, experts in the Law and religious leaders, more than anyone else. In Matthew 23, for example, he warned his followers that these leaders did not practice what they preached. They seized divine honors for themselves when "they do all their deeds to be

---

10. Marguerite Shuster, *The Fall and Sin: What We Have Become as Sinners* (Grand Rapids: Eerdmans, 2004), 51.

seen by others. For they make their phylacteries broad and their fringes long, and they love the place of honor at feasts and the best seats in the synagogues and greetings in the marketplaces and being called rabbi by others" (vv. 5–7). Then he concluded, "The greatest among you shall be your servant. Whoever exalts himself will be humbled, and whoever humbles himself will be exalted" (vv. 11–12). As we proceed through the Bible, the ethical antithesis between pride/degradation and humility/exaltation will be our constant companion.

In psychological terms, Adam and Eve recognized their nakedness as a shameful exposure of their new alienation from God and one another. They tried to cover their shame (Gen. 3:7), but their opened eyes gave them an experiential awareness of evil that could be healed only by the gracious provision of God (v. 22). The condition of human life thereafter was not obedience to the Word but rather a rebellion that has militated against an understanding of self as a creature of God. As Josef Pieper stated,

> Pride refers to man's relationship to God. Pride is the anti-realistic denial of the relationship between creature and Creator; pride denies the creaturely nature of man.... It is a turning away from God. And this is more pronounced in pride than in any other sin.... Humility, too, looks first to God ... Humility, as "subjection of man to God," is the affirmation of this essential and primordial fact.[11]

The couple fearfully tried to hide from God, thus indicating their loss of relationship with him (v. 8). "Where are you?" the LORD God called, forcing them to face their rebellion, "Have you eaten from the tree of which I commanded you not to eat?" (v. 11). The man answered, "I was afraid, because I was naked; and I

---

11. Josef Pieper, *The Four Cardinal Virtues*, trans. Daniel Coogan (South Bend, IN: University of Notre Dame, 1966), 191.

hid myself" (v. 10). Thus, Gerhard Von Rad correctly observes, "If shame was the sign of a disturbance of man's relation to other men, then fear before God was a sign of a disorder in his relation to his Creator. Fear and shame are henceforth the incurable stigmata of the Fall in man."[12] Finally, the fall triggered the couple's sense of guilt, so that they blamed God, the woman, and Satan respectively (vv. 12–13). The deception of the serpent had now saturated the human condition (cf. Jer. 17:9).[13]

The creational mandate to rule under God was cursed with the pain of childbirth and toilsome labor until sinners returned to the dust of death (Gen. 3:16–19). Pain in life is shared by both men and women, and the tragic consequence of the situation is seen in the curse of death: "till you return to the ground, for out of it you were taken; for you are dust, and to dust you shall return" (v. 19). A mere creature from clay had aspired to be God! In the words of Vernon Grounds, "Despite his dignity, therefore, his inestimable worth as *imago dei*, man as a finite agent of rebellion is indeed 'dust and ashes.'"[14] Now the fact of death has overshadowed all of life; a memory of paradise has been entangled in a hopeless struggle with ongoing evil and inevitable death. As ruling husband in God's creational order, Adam names the woman "Eve" as the mother of human life. However, only with the Creator's gracious garments of skin could life continue outside of the garden, anticipating the principle that blood must be shed for the forgiveness of sin (cf. Heb. 9:22).[15] And only after

12. Gerhard Von Rad, *Genesis: A Commentary*, rev. ed., trans. John Marks, OTL (Philadelphia: Westminster, 1972), 91.

13. A more familiar designation for our corporate condition is *flesh* or *sin nature* (*sarx*; cf. Gal. 5:19–21).

14. *Zondervan Pictorial Encyclopedia of the Bible*, ed. Merrill C. Tenney (Grand Rapids: Zondervan, 1975), s.v. "Humility," by Vernon Grounds.

15. Collins, *Genesis 1–4*, 215n61, argues that the verse does not mention sacrifice and contains no technical vocabulary that would point in that direction. It is true that the first mention of sacrifice occurs in Genesis 4:3–4, but 3:21 may refer to God's replacement of "their pathetic fig-leaf loincloths with something more durable, more

the gracious advent of the Son of Man could creation's curse be reversed to the everlasting praise of the Creator.

Fallen dominion is presented next as Cain murders Abel, submitting to sin "crouching at the door. Its desire is for you, but you must rule over it" (Gen. 4:7). In this verse sin is personified as an animal, a subhuman creature as the serpent had been. God warned Cain to subdue it, as Adam and Eve should have done. Like his parents, he failed.[16] Abel's blood cried to God, who cursed the ground, forcing Cain to become a "restless wanderer on the earth."[17] The first couple, then Cain, and later Israel would be expelled to experience exile apart from a place of blessing. Without a stable and secure home, he was fearful that "whoever finds me will kill me" (v. 14). As such, he represents the insecurity of fallen humanity for whom death is an ever-present reality (cf. Rom. 6:23). To find security apart from

---

suited to the hard lives they will face outside the garden" (ibid., 175). However, Collins is correct as well in noting, "The special meeting place between God and his people is now the sanctuary, in public worship, with its sacramental rites that address our guilt" (ibid., 154n26). Gordon Wenham prefers the meaning "priestly decency": "Here again the terminology of the garden of Eden runs closely parallel to the vocabulary associated with worship in the tabernacle. . . . It therefore follows that in Eden, the garden of God, men and women must be decently clad, so God clothes them himself." *Genesis 1–15*, WBC 1 (Nashville: Nelson, 1987), 1:84. On the other hand, the *ESV Study Bible*'s note on the verse supports a sacrificial reference: "Because God provides garments to clothe Adam and Eve, thus requiring the death of an animal to cover their nakedness, many see a parallel here related to (1) the system of animal sacrifices to atone for sin later instituted by God through the leadership of Moses in Israel, and (2) the eventual sacrificial death of Christ as an atonement for sin." *ESV Study Bible* (Wheaton, IL: Crossway, 2001), 57, s.v. "Genesis 3:21."

16. "Cain goes 'away from the presence of the LORD'; verses 17–24 show that this departure is not a matter of place but of moral orientation." Collins, *Genesis 1–4*, 212. Note 1 John 3:12 for validation of the judgment on Cain's character.

17. *Blood* may be rendered in the plural with the implication that Cain had no regard for Abel's descendants as well, hence in the fratricide he doubly proved that he was not his "brother's keeper." Leon Kass emphasizes the extent of the consequences: "Not just the will of Abel, but the cosmos itself has been violated; the crime is a crime against 'blood'—against life and kin; the whole earth, polluted and stained with bloodshed, cries in anguish and for retribution." *The Beginning of Wisdom: Reading Genesis* (New York: Free Press, 2003), 142–43.

God, Cain built Enoch, where technical accomplishments fostered pride among the city's inhabitants (Gen. 4:17–22). Another descendant, Lamech, exemplified the family's characteristic presumption with his bigamous taunt in defiance of marriage and his vengeful abuse of dominion (vv. 23–24), which extended even to the murder of a boy. Lamech demonstrated that fallen image bearers are still capable of impressive achievements, which can be evil or beneficial, depending on the orientation of the person toward God.

Lamech's pride compounded until mankind's wickedness was pervasive, and "every intention of the thoughts of his heart was only evil continually" (Gen. 6:5). The terminology points to a persistently willful rebellion against God. The encompassing wickedness corrupted humanity and filled the earth with violence (v. 11). The notion of corruption meant that the population of the time had rendered themselves useless for righteous rule over creation. So the LORD, filled with grief, resolved to "blot out man whom I have created from the face of the land" (v. 7). Once again, the connection between sin and death is unmistakable.

The emphasis on pervasive evil makes one wonder about God and his earlier decree and provision for Adam and Eve. The decree was unconditional, so God gave the honor of preserving life in the dying world to a few humble families, who walked obediently with him in spite of the depraved crowds. One can hardly overemphasize that the Creator's plan would go forward with his chosen people rather than humanity in general—a fact that underscores obedience as the biblical way of blessing. This progression is seen in that the first couple had other children named Seth and Enosh, and from their families "people began to call upon the name of the LORD" (Gen. 4:26).[18] From this righteous

18. Genesis 5:1–2 points us back to 1:26–28, which ties Seth's line to God's creational will that will be perpetuated through godly families. The name is the covenantal name, meaning that Seth's descendants will live in relational obedience to God.

line came Enoch,[19] who faithfully walked with God (5:22–23). In spite of his context, Enoch was characterized by submission to the LORD. Apparently because of his righteousness, and perhaps to deliver him from the violence of his day, God prematurely elevated Enoch to his presence without death (cf. Heb. 11:5).[20]

Why do righteous lines usually seem to be so few in number? Why has the world not witnessed masses of people becoming righteous and inclining their thoughts to God's glory? Genesis 5 seems to indicate a succession of families over long periods of time, who apparently "call[ed] on the name of the LORD." We must realize, however, that comparatively few believers turn their backs on renown to walk sacrificially with God. How many people have lived like Noah's family, who were the only survivors of the flood? We know that God graciously exalts his humble believers, and that they, like Abel, still speak through the Scriptures millennia after their deaths (cf. Heb. 11:4). We also know that wicked multitudes have passed into a dusty oblivion. What gave the families of Seth, Enoch, and Noah the stamina and courage to walk with the LORD in their wicked generations? I would suggest that their close relationships with God gave them the wisdom that humble submission to his Word is the pathway of grace, honor, and life.

My friend Wayne evidenced that this kind of commitment is as true today as it was then. He learned to walk with God through Bible studies while he was in the Navy. At Moody Bible

---

19. The Enoch descended from Seth was not Cain's son, who had the same name. The common names *Enoch* and *Lamech* reflect the power of faith to form divergent characters. "It [the literary effect] leads us to note that the decline we see in Cain's family was not an inevitable outcome of being human; rather it flowed from the moral orientation of the members, which in turn is influenced by the orientation of the head member of the list." Collins, *Genesis 1–4*, 201.

20. Jude 14 uses the testimony of Enoch before the flood to prefigure judgment against godlessness in the future. Godless people are characterized as followers of their own evil desires; "they are loud-mouthed boasters, showing favoritism to gain advantage" (v. 16).

Institute his ministries taught him that "he'd rather see a sermon than hear one any day. I'd rather one would walk with me than merely point the way." With his wife, Betty, he devoted his life to biblical translation among the Machiguenga people in Peru. A consistent and unpretentious Christian, he faithfully encouraged fellow believers until cancer elevated him to the presence of the Lord at a ripe old age. I asked him how he lived above the pressures of the world. He simply responded that he turned his eyes on Jesus, and the things of earth grew strangely dim. That seems to be the chorus of Enoch-like saints through the ages; their focus on the things of God keeps them from the self-destructive corruptions around them.

At the time of the flood, Noah was born to comfort his family in their arduous labor on the ground that the LORD had cursed (Gen. 5:29). Like Enoch, Noah humbly walked with God, "a righteous man, blameless in his generation" (6:9; cf. 7:1). This initial use of *righteousness* in the Bible refers to both covenant relationship and proper conduct.[21] Allen Ross summarizes Noah's righteousness as "conforming to the requirements of the relationship he had with God."[22] Consequently, his trust in the Word set him apart from the violence of his generation. He "found favor in the eyes of the LORD," who blessed him with the continuation of humanity (6:8).

The first use of the word *covenant* in the Bible occurs with God's promise to his creation as represented by Noah (Gen. 9:8–17). This promise's connection with his decree in 1:28 is obvious. They were to be fruitful, and the family's dominion would cause fear in lower creatures on the earth (9:1–2). Although God gave mankind everything for food, they could not partake of blood

---

21. Righteousness is connected with obedience in: Ezekiel 14:14, 23; Hebrews 11:7; 1 Peter 3:20; and 2 Peter 2:5.

22. Allen P. Ross, *Creation and Blessing: A Guide to the Study and Exposition of Genesis* (Grand Rapids: Baker Books, 1988), 193.

or shed the blood of another person (vv. 4–6). God's requirement of death for killers protected humanity from extinction, and the rainbow signed his commitment to life forever unto the advent of the eternal new heavens and earth. The promise was expressed in terms of his everlasting memory, which imprinted generations from the call of Abram to the advent of Messiah, who was born in the lineage of the patriarchs.

The depravity of mankind emerged again in the second universal rebellion at Shinar, when "the whole world had one language and a common speech" (Gen. 11:1, NIV). Shinar was the region of imperial cities in Mesopotamia, which exemplified the pride of the assembled settlers (cf. 10:8–10). Their resolve was to make bricks from the clay, to build a city with a tower that reached to the heavens (cf. 4:17). In other words, they would use the clay, from which they came, to build a monument that would challenge God and visualize their fear of wandering over the face of the earth.

Enuma Elish, the Babylonian creation epic, records the building of Babylon from the Mesopotamian perspective. Its remarkable parallels with the Genesis narrative indicate that the Bible is arguing against Babylon's idolatry and its pride-inspired structures. They refer to a comprehensive sense of pride that has been labeled as hubris, Titanism, or overweening presumption. Their idolatry was self-worship, since their dead idols were merely the projected values of sinful people. This is further indicated by the emphatic use of the first person in their resolve: "us," "ourselves," "us," "ourselves," and "we" (Gen. 11:4). This narcissistic preoccupation can easily slide into a love and praise of self rather than God. As such, it repeated the initial attempt to be God (3:22), making pride a noxious form of idolatry. A hatred of insignificance and fear of worthlessness drive people to spectacular aspirations and efforts. Their hope is that the anticipated attainments may immortalize them in history. In the process they seize glory that belongs to God alone and exploit other people for their own ends.

The Babylonian account stands in contrast to Genesis. The patron deity Marduk "glowed with pleasure" over the impressive brickwork, which would be named "The Sanctuary." The gods "raised high the head" of the temple tower to the heavens, the lifting of the head with haughty eyes being an image of pride.[23] Babylon was portrayed as a celestial city that established the supremacy of Marduk over all deities as a reflection of its own preeminence on earth. The underlying purpose of its builders was to "make a name for ourselves lest we be dispersed over the face of the whole earth" (Gen. 11:4). Their labor for a great name meant fame or renown. Instead of filling the earth as God's ambassadors (cf. 9:1), they sought to build a titanic symbol by which they could godlessly dominate God's creation (cf. 6:4). The city was to be a sign of their aggressive self-reliance, and the tower symbolized their will to fame. The generation at Babel parallels the flood generation and reaffirms an endemic arrogance in sinful humanity.

God, on the other hand, "came down" (Gen. 11:5) to see the comparatively puny city and tower, which satirically reduced the human bid for godless greatness to insignificance. God's own self-deliberation affirmed the extraordinary abilities of humanity by noting that a godless kingdom would be accessible to them, as demonstrated throughout history (v. 6). However, they were only people, who deluded themselves with heavenly goals in rebellion against God. He resolved to judge their wicked thoughts and plans by confusing their language, which canceled their ability to understand one another. Their intent to disobey God's command resulted in their own chaotic scattering over the whole earth, as reflected in the genealogies of Genesis 10.

23. James B. Pritchard, ed., *Ancient Near Eastern Texts Relating to the Old Testament*, 3rd ed. (Princeton: Princeton University Press, 1950), 68–69.

The lessons of the encounter between the settlers and God are central to the Bible. Babel became Babylon, an imperial monster that mirrored the fallen world (cf. Isa. 13–14; Jer. 50–51; and Rev. 17–18). John's Revelation pictured the bricks as sins, which will crumble in a culminating judgment of God (18:5). Then the New Jerusalem will come down from heaven, the true celestial city, and God will dwell with his people forever (21:2–3). Israel needed to learn that God curses human ambitions for godless significance and security. The heaviness of the temptation to disobey God can be seen in the Israelites' repeated attempts to win the approval of empires by compromising their allegiance to the Lord. Each Israelite, like us, needed to remember that faithful obedience to the Word brings lasting blessing from the Lord.

Humility as God-Centeredness

Again, judgment was followed by the Lord's gracious call of Abram to leave his country and household to go to the land (Canaan) that God would show him (Gen. 12:1; cf. 9:24–27). God promised that he would ultimately use Abram's family to bring salvation to all the families of the earth (12:3). Humility is implied, rather than explicitly stated, in Abram's obedience and pilgrimage to receive God's blessings of land, name, and children (vv. 2–3; 13:15–17). We should note that the gift of "a great name" stands in stark contrast to the Babylonian ambition for a name. Abraham is a clear example of God blessing his faithful followers with lasting fame beyond their comprehension. God's covenant in chapter 15 underscores his grace and Abram's faith in the relationship (v. 6). The Lord considered Abram righteous because he believed the Word and humbly accepted divine directions in his life. Even though Abram and Sarai were imperfect in instances like Hagar and Ishmael (16:1), God commanded Abram to "walk before me, and be blameless" (17:1) and reconfirmed his covenant.

He gave Abram and Sarai new names as a personal guarantee of his promises. "Abram" signified a distinguished lineage, but "Abraham" in wordplay became a perpetual reminder that he was to be "father of a multitude." Sarai became Sarah, who as "princess" would be the mother of kings to come. The issue was not perfection but rather obedience to the Word in worshipful recognition of God's presence and promise.[24]

Consequently, the aged couple was blessed miraculously with Isaac (21:1–5). Abraham supremely demonstrated humility before the LORD in his willingness to sacrifice his beloved son. The "LORD Will Provide" acknowledged the demonstration with a stunning promise:

> I will surely bless you, and I will surely multiply your offspring
> as the stars of heaven and as the sand that is on the seashore.
> And your offspring shall possess the gate of his enemies, and
> in your offspring shall all the nations of the earth be blessed,
> because you have obeyed my voice. (22:17–18)

When God called Abraham to willingly return the heir of the promises to his Giver, the patriarch's obedience exemplified the worship of a humble heart. He illustrated that biblical sacrifice is a gift of the best that we have, which in the New Testament becomes our lives, indeed ourselves: "I appeal to you therefore, brothers, by the mercies of God, to present your bodies as a living sacrifice, holy and acceptable to God, which is your spiritual worship" (Rom. 12:1). This is humility in its most practical expression, which enables us to live without thinking more highly of

---

24. Jacob, though deceitful earlier, exemplifies a humbled person in life's threatening circumstances: "I am not worthy of the least of all the deeds of steadfast love and all the faithfulness that you have shown to your servant, for with only my staff I crossed this Jordan, and now I have become two camps. Please deliver me from the hand of my brother" (Gen. 32:10–11).

ourselves than we ought to think (v. 3), acknowledging that our effectiveness is a gift from God. It reflects the example of the Trinity, in which the Father "so loved the world" that he gave his only Son, through the Spirit, for our salvation.

Humility is the daily gift of our ambitions and our abilities to God for his glory, trusting him for our needs and personal significance. In a self-interested culture Abraham's sacrifice seems to be far removed from our concerns about profits and life-consuming desires for a "successful name," whatever that means. Noah floated through the flood, but how do I please God as I struggle with the mud puddles of my life? As I have considered my "living sacrifice," I have consulted my files of reminders of how God has blessed me through my serving others: Bill's note of thanks for lunch and prayer during his struggle with a personal failure; another friend's thanks for prayer for a dying relative; a thank-you for my hospital visit after cancer surgery; another friend's gratitude for a little money that paid a debt in time of need. The notes remind me that real life is much deeper than public applause. From Adam to Abraham, humility is best exhibited in personal faithfulness—often with no return except the grateful heart of a fellow pilgrim and God's pleasure as indicated in his Word. Interestingly, these little things become the big things that characterize a significant faith in the Lord.

The initial chapters of Genesis placed humility as obedience to the Word at the center of God's creation and life on earth. Pride and humility from the beginning have been opposing attitudes evidenced by faith in or rebellion against the Word. The vice and virtue are presented in a setting of central concerns for all human beings as unique creatures on earth, thereby focusing on God as the ultimate arbiter of human behavior: life and death, righteousness and sin, and moral choice. Genesis 1–11 is thoroughly God-centered. "In the beginning God . . ." should permeate Christian theology. This means that people must be viewed as dignified creatures under our Creator and sin is essentially pride rebelling against creaturely limitations. The seriousness of sin is that it is deadly insubordination against God. Only in this perspective can we begin to comprehend God's interview in the garden, his grief at the flood, his condescension to judge Babel, and the grievous unnaturalness of the deaths of our family and friends. The initial temptation was to rebel against creaturely dependence on the Creator, and two developments toward pervasive rebellion demonstrate that the fallen human condition is characterized by pride. The genealogical refrains of chapters 5 and 11 drum the reality of the fallen world: "and he died."

On the other hand, God's grace in the lives of Enoch, Noah, and Abram demonstrate that God honors his Word by exalting humble believers. As his Word preserved his creational will through his people, so God humbled unbelievers unto death as emphasized in the judgments of the flood and Babel. The names of godly believers are still honored by the family of God, but depraved cities and empires have evaporated into the dust of death. From Adam to Abraham the consequences of pride versus humility are testimonies about God's ways on earth. Strangely, people persist in rejecting God as the Standard until they humbly submit to his loving grace.

We have also seen that Genesis addresses two crucial issues that give us wisdom about godly living in a fallen world. First, the chapters present a view of humanity that reflects our aggressive nature. We were made to rule. Everyone lives for or against God, not as passive pawns in a fatalistic world or as neutral creatures trying to find their way in hostile, bewildering options. Biblically, pride is aggression against God (or disobedience, such as Cain and the settlers at Babel), while humility is ambition for God's glory (or serving him like the families of Enoch, Noah, and Abraham). Second, the chapters teach us that the fall resulted in both the corruption of human rule and the utter need for God's grace for life to continue on earth. Grace is the living hope for the world, which mandates careful attention to biblical wisdom. Commenting on a deluge of ethical failures in 2008, Martin Marty observed, "The witness to broken trust is so vast and deep that to avoid it would be irresponsible."[25] He is correct, and other years in recent memory could be similarly summarized, at least in my seven decades on earth. Yes, we may have retained our abilities to build cities and govern societies, but our God-given, technical prowess is accompanied by moral decline and misuse of God's gracious blessings. We should honestly acknowledge man's wickedness on the earth, and, at the same time, we should recognize that our desire to know God leads us "as by rivulets to the spring [of God's grace]."[26]

Moses as an Example of Humility in Israel

The light of grace brilliantly transformed a darkened heart into a humble servant in the case of Moses. Although he had received a princely education in Egypt, Moses was an exile shepherding his flock in remote Horeb when the LORD called him to deliver Israel from the arrogant Egyptian empire (Ex. 18:11; cf. Neh. 9:10). Moses spoke for the LORD, the God of the Hebrews, when he asked Pharaoh, "How long will you refuse to humble yourself before me?" (Ex. 10:3). His faithfulness in his leadership over Israel gave him the preeminent privilege of knowing the LORD "face to face" (Deut. 34:10).

About six hundred years after the birth of Isaac, Moses was leading the Israelites from Sinai to Kadesh (Num. 10:11–12:16).

---

25. Martin E. Marty, "On Trust," Sightings, Religion News Service, December 22, 2008.

26. Calvin, *Institutes*, 1.1.1. He states, "No one can look upon himself without immediately turning his thoughts to the contemplation of God, in whom he 'lives and moves' [Acts 17:28]" (ibid.).

Rebellion and judgment characterized the journey. The Israelites complained about hardships, and the LORD judged them with fire (11:1–3). In response to their cries, Moses prayed and God extinguished the fire. Instigated by "rabble," the Israelites again complained about manna and requested meat out of their flawed memory of Egyptian delicacies (vv. 4–6). As Moses listened to their wailing, he lamented to God:

> Where am I to get meat to give to all this people? For they weep before me and say, "Give us meat that we may eat." I am not able to carry all this people alone; the burden is too heavy for me. If you will treat me like this, kill me at once, if I find favor in your sight, that I may not see my wretchedness. (11:13–15)

Moses' admission that he was not able, because the burden was too heavy, was a humble plea for God's gracious intervention. In response, the LORD called for seventy leaders, whom he gifted with the Spirit. Eldad and Medad, perhaps among the chosen elders, missed the convocation at the tent of meeting and prophesied elsewhere in the camp (vv. 16–30). Joshua sought to disqualify them, but a grateful Moses responded, "Would that all the LORD's people were prophets, that the LORD would put his Spirit on them!" (v. 29). Nevertheless, the LORD caused a wind to blow an abundance of quail into the camp, which resulted in a plague among the people (vv. 31–34). Rebellion against God's mediator is arrogance toward God himself.

After the fire and plague, Miriam and Aaron rebelled against their brother's leadership (Num. 12:1). Miriam seems to have been the instigator of the complaint, as indicated by the verbal form (feminine singular), the placement of her name before Aaron, and the severity of her judgment. Aaron seems to have been easily persuaded to join sinful behavior (cf. Ex. 32:1–6, 21–24).

Their initial charge was that Moses had married a Cushite

woman. The accusation suggests that his first wife had died, and Moses had remarried a non-Hebrew. The charge was obviously a pretense, since their real concern was Moses' privileged relationship with God: "Has the Lord indeed spoken only through Moses? Has he not spoken through us also?" (Num. 12:2). That privileged relationship raised the contextual issue of Moses' unique prophetic status and suggests the legitimacy of their voices as well.[27] Their problem was envy, a self-centered vice that flows from pride. Miriam and Aaron had been blessed with significant leadership, so their envy was unwarranted. Micah recalled that the three of them had been key leaders in the exodus: "For I brought you up from the land of Egypt and redeemed you from the house of slavery, and I sent before you Moses, Aaron, and Miriam" (Mic. 6:4). Miriam, in particular, had led a chorus of praise after Israel's deliverance: "Then Miriam, the prophetess, the sister of Aaron, took a tambourine in her hand, and all the women went out after her with tambourines and dancing" (Ex. 15:20). The Israelites' unrest and the judgments of God had no doubt raised public questions about Moses' leadership. Joshua's attempt to silence Eldad and Medad may have reflected a larger concern that Moses had bypassed important people for gifted leadership of the nation (Num. 11:16, 24–29). Miriam and Aaron's use of "us" points to wounded pride and dissatisfaction with God's sovereign direction during the wilderness sojourn. "And the Lord heard it" (12:2) marks God's intention to suddenly intervene in behalf of his special servant. He summoned the accusers to come forward with Moses at the tent of meeting.

Numbers 12:3 is a literary aside to underscore the accusation's absurdity: "Now the man Moses was very meek, more than all the

27. Moses, burdened by the leadership of the nation, had rebuked Joshua for requesting that Eldad and Medad be silenced: "Are you jealous for my sake? I wish that all the Lord's people were prophets, and that the Lord would put his Spirit on them!" (Num. 11:29, NIV).

people who were on the face of the earth." Ronald Allen wrote that this "is the most difficult line in the chapter, and one of the most difficult verses in the entire book."[28] Moses may have been exasperated, but he did not seem to be humble in the sense that we understand the virtue—namely, self-depreciating and retiring. I suggest that the meaning of the verse can be found in the LORD's explanation (vv. 6–7) and an understanding of biblical humility. Although Moses had admitted his frustrations with the people, he was aware that their rebellious attitudes were directed against God and that, as mediator, he was caught in the crosshairs of the conflict.

The word translated "meek" or "humble" (עָנָו) comes from a concept meaning lowliness or submission.[29] The term is related to another word (עָנִי) that refers to an afflicted person who has been humbled by difficult circumstances. On the contrary, the concept for "arrogance" (גָּאוֹן) refers to a haughty attitude that resembles an uncontrollable wave, sweeping away people and structures in its path. Arrogance is a presumptuous view of self that promotes chaos in its callous disregard of both God and other people, like the so-called leaders who crushed Ron and Betty's dreams in the mortgage crisis. Although arrogance can refer to God with a positive sense of his exalted glory, its reference to people negatively refers to self-glorification. Lamech's twisted taunt about his ungodly fame is a noteworthy example. Sin comes into play at the shift from submission to God to self-assertion—trying to gain what rightfully belongs to the

28. Ronald Allen, *Numbers*, ed. Frank E. Gaebelein et al, EBC 2 (Grand Rapids: Zondervan, 1990), 798. The hermeneutical difficulty of the verse stems from the meaning of עָנָו and the coherency of Numbers 12 as a literary unit. Alternative meanings of the term include "afflicted," "meek," and "honorable." Cf. John Dickson and Brian Rosner, "Humility as a Social Virtue in the Hebrew Bible?," *Vetus Testamentum* 54 (2004): 459–79.

29. If there is a distinction between meekness and humility, then the former connotes gentleness or submissiveness while the latter has to do with social status or estimation. The terms are related, and any distinction should not be overly emphasized.

Lord. As D. H. Tongue wrote, "Rebellious pride, which refuses to depend on God and be subject to Him, but attributes to self the honour due to Him, figures as the very root and essence of sin."[30] Philip Budd interprets Numbers 12:3 with a similar emphasis: "The point here seems to be that Moses is not self-assertive. His uniqueness is something conferred by God."[31] Therefore, humility in Scripture is a very positive concept related to honoring God in daily circumstances rather than just a man-centered virtue: "In the OT, then, we find no glorifying of self-abasement. There is prophetic criticism of fasting customs and stress is laid on the proper attitude of the heart to God and his will."[32] In simplest terms one might conclude that humility is godly service, while pride is aggression for self. These meanings satisfy the unusual description of Moses as the humblest man on earth.

Humility is not about Moses' personality or character traits as much as his faithfulness among the people and his earnestness about the LORD's presence (cf. Ex. 33:12–23). The episodes show a prideful resistance to God's direction, and Moses was noticeably humble, because he faithfully obeyed the LORD and prayed for his contentious flock. He prayed for relief from the judgmental fire, and the LORD honored his intercession (Num. 11:2). He prayed about the peoples' desire for meat, and the LORD provided quail and lightened his burden with gifted elders (vv. 24–25). He did not vengefully retaliate against Miriam and Aaron but prayed that God would heal his errant sister (12:13).

Moses was not only "very meek" but also more humble "than all people who were on the face of the earth" (Num. 12:3).[33] If humility is understood in terms of one's relationship with God,

30. J. D. Douglas, ed., *New Bible Dictionary* (Grand Rapids: Eerdmans, 1962), s.v. "Pride," by D. H. Tongue, 1027.
31. Philip Budd, *Numbers*, vol. 5 of WBC 5 (Waco, TX: Word, 1984), 136.
32. *TNDT*, s.v. "*tapeinós ktl*," by Walter Grundmann.
33. The assertion is one of incomparability, adding preeminence to Moses' prophetic calling as in Deuteronomy 34:10: "There has not arisen a prophet since in Israel like

then Moses was the unique mediator between the one and only living Creator and his chosen nation (cf. Deut. 7:7–8). In other words, Moses' humility was measured by God's greatness. He represented the Lord before the Egyptian emperor, led the Israelites to Sinai, organized the nation according to the Law, and directed Israel's defeat of enemies in the wilderness. These accomplishments were all carried out as the Lord commanded him (cf. Ex. 34), an obedience to the Presence who had enabled him from the beginning (cf. Ex. 3–4). God, of course, had made himself known through prophetic visions and dreams, but with Moses he spoke "mouth to mouth, clearly, and not in riddles, and [Moses] beholds the form of the Lord" (Num. 12:8). In other words, the Lord spoke personally and directly with his unique servant. This understanding of humility as a prophetic dependence on God and his Word is emphasized by Richard Briggs:

> We shall examine the text . . . and argue that the kind of understanding of humility required to make sense of this verse relies on the primary importance of dependence upon God. . . . I want to suggest that what sets Moses apart as the most humble person on the earth is defined in this passage as his unique status as a recipient of God's spoken word "face to face." In other words, humility, as depicted in this narrative, is dependence upon God, and in particular, it is dependence upon God for any speaking of a divinely authorized word.[34]

Briggs uses God-centeredness to refer to "a category of relatedness" rather than meekness. He prefers "preeminence" rather

---

Moses, whom the Lord knew face to face." Extrabiblical literature tended to divinize Moses because of his extraordinary relationship with God. Prescient is the descriptive "the man Moses" in Numbers 12:3 before his "elevation" over the others.

34. Richard S. Briggs, *The Virtuous Reader: Old Testament Narrative and Interpretive Virtue* (Grand Rapids: Baker Academic, 2010), 49, 60.

than "uniqueness" to allow for continuity in Israel's tradition in which prophets spoke vigorously, yet respectfully, with the Lord.

Moses was set apart by God's sovereign discretion and was faithful albeit fallible, as the latter part of Numbers indicates (20:1–13). True to his covenantal principles, God exalted his humble servant and vindicated him with the countercharge, "Why then were you not afraid to speak against my servant Moses?" (12:8). God claimed, in effect, that to oppose Moses was to reject the Lord himself.

When the cloud receded from the tent, Aaron and Moses observed that Miriam was leprous. Her infectious skin disease required her exclusion from the camp for seven days (cf. Num. 5:1–4). Aaron's plea for mercy prompted Moses to pray for her healing (12:11–13). God responded that she had shamed her family, so she must be publicly excluded to demonstrate that God opposes the proud.

As we reflect on the incident, it may seem that this public humiliation was disproportionate to Miriam's seemingly insignificant sin. We recall the same issue when Adam and Eve's mere disobedience resulted in the fall of humanity. In response, we should first note that Miriam's sin was an act of rebellion against God, exposing that our values can be quite different from God's standard, which is our humble acceptance of his Word and will. Biblical justice makes sense only in light of the reality of the divine Judge; our canons of justice make sense only in light of a consensus of our collective will. Both systems are designed to maintain public order, although modern justice often seems to promote chaos with its fluid standards. The existence of God necessarily requires that some laws are social absolutes if large numbers of people are to live together in unity.

Second, we should note that Miriam's sin was a public sin, which required public consequences. The Israelites' propensity to rebellion meant that they would have interpreted a tolerant attitude as license to bring the nation's pilgrimage to a halt, if they were so inclined. Later, consistent with the principle of public discipline, the LORD punished Moses. "Because you did not believe in me, to uphold me as holy in the eyes of the people of Israel, therefore you shall not bring this assembly into the land that I have given them" (Num. 20:12). Moses was commanded to merely speak to the rock for water, which underscored the presence of God in Israel's midst. When he instead struck the rock, he publicly disobeyed God's Word and claimed credit for the miracle (v. 10). From this perspective Miriam's punishment matched her sinful accusation, and "the people did not set out on the march until Miriam was brought in again" (12:15). God strictly opposes pride!

Moses' Prediction of Pride in Israel

As Deuteronomy began Moses led the Israelites to the plains of Moab across from Jericho, and at the end of the book they were still there (34:8). Their journey to the land had been interrupted in Numbers as the lawgiver exhorted the nation to remember the past and the people prepared for their entry under Joshua's leadership. Deuteronomy 8 has much to say about humility, as Moses calls the nation to obedience with the paired themes of remembrance/forgetfulness and wilderness/promised land. The chapter's emphasis resembles the nuance of humility in Numbers 12:3. It begins with an exhortation to obey the Word "that you may live and multiply, and go in and possess the land that the LORD swore to give to your fathers" (Deut. 8:1). Moses described obedience as "walking in [God's] ways and . . . fearing him" (v. 6). In particular, the Israelites were to remember how the LORD had cared for them for forty years in the wilderness. God's purpose in their hardships had been to "humble you, testing you to know what was in your heart, whether you would keep his commandments or not" (v. 2). The desolate environment had reduced the people to trusting God for common needs like food, clothing, and health. They were constantly reminded that their survival depended on their loving relationship with the living God: "He humbled you and let you hunger and fed you with manna, which you did not know, nor did your fathers know, that he might make you know that man does not live by bread alone, but man lives by every word that comes from the mouth of the LORD" (v. 3). As mentioned elsewhere in the Pentateuch, humility meant an obedient walk with the LORD rather than an independent attitude of self-sufficiency.

God's discipline was to teach Israel a basic covenantal principle in life: "man does not live by bread alone, but man lives by every word that comes from the mouth of the LORD" (Deut. 8:3). This did not mean that the Israelites did not need sustenance or that they were to expect miraculous provisions like manna in every circumstance. It meant that they were to learn that God is the basic source of life, and his commands implicitly promised his provisions for their needs. In other words, bread alone is not sufficient for the relational needs of loving God with all of one's heart (cf. Deut. 4:29).

The lesson was reinforced on another occasion when Jesus was tempted by the devil in a wilderness (Matt. 4:1–11). Weary and hungry after fasting for forty days, he resisted miracles of bread, endured life-threatening risks, and rejected idolatry with quotations from Deuteronomy 8:3; 6:16; and 6:13 respectively. He demonstrated that dependence on God's provision is sufficient for even the most difficult challenges. From any angle, this is one of the hardest lessons for us to learn. We must work for our daily needs, but we must realize that God graciously enables our labors. In Peter Craigie's words, "Man knows that he must work in order to provide the essentials for physical existence, but in that very labor, he may easily forget that, in the last resort, it is

God who makes provision for man's life."[35] James underscored this point when he asked,

> What is your life? For you are a mist that appears for a little time and then vanishes. Instead you ought to say, "If the Lord wills, we will live and do this or that." As it is, you boast in your arrogance. All such boasting is evil. (4:14–16)

The virtue of humble dependence dissipates the pride of self-sufficiency.

A second biblical principle concerns the familial love of God for his children: "Know then in your heart that, as a man disciplines his son, the LORD your God disciplines you" (Deut. 8:5; cf. Prov. 3:11–12; Heb. 12:5–6). Far from being capricious, God's severe tests and trials were all prompted by his loving plan to plant the Israelites prosperously in the land.

The goodness of God in his gift of the land is described poetically in Deuteronomy 8:7–10, and this passage is followed by a striking insight about biblical pride and humility. In stark contrast to the wilderness, the promised land was a place with abundant water, bountiful harvests, and a wealth of minerals. In such a place Israel was to "take care lest you forget the LORD your God by not keeping his commandments" (v. 11). Pride is defined as forgetting God, as indicated by failure to obey his commands. It is a lifting up of one's heart in pride of accomplishment rather than blessing the LORD for his gifts.

This insight is introduced by Moses' prescient awareness that the Israelites will prosper in the land with satisfied appetites, fine homes, and multiplying wealth. Humility before the Lord will be lost at their time of greatest success! Their hearts will become proud and boast. "Beware lest you say in your heart, 'My

35. Peter Craigie, *The Book of Deuteronomy*, NICOT, 186.

power and the might of my hand have gotten me this wealth'" (Deut. 8:17). The boast will ignore the exodus from slavery, the divine provision of food and water, and protection from fearsome creatures like serpents and scorpions. J. A. Thompson noted, "To forget these facts was to display base ingratitude and self-deifying pride."[36] Their sin would ignore the discipline of God, who had tested them "to do you good in the end" (v. 16). Moses continued, "Remember the LORD your God, for it is he who gives you power to get wealth" (v. 18).

The force of the chapter lies in two implications of the Old Testament's notion of remembering. First, memory involved both recall and response. Timothy Ashley cautioned that remembering "does not mean simply bringing something to mind, but using whatever means necessary to make real in the present what was real in the past: the power and love of Yahweh shown in statutes and ordinances for the guidance of his people (cf. Deut. 6:24; 10:13). Remembering in this sense includes doing."[37] Thus, the memory and its celebration were designed to perpetuate a living tradition whereby future generations could dwell on the covenantal goodness of God as a motivation for faithfulness in their lives (cf. Deut. 4:9). According to Craigie, "Forgetfulness is not simply a state of mind, or something akin to absentmindedness. Facts may still be remembered, in a literal sense, but they have ceased to be part of a living memory of the reality of God, who no longer seems to be a living and real presence."[38] This living memory was necessary for the maintenance of humility as an obedient reverence for God, even when his commands were not fully understood.

---

36. J. A. Thompson, *Deuteronomy*, TOTC, 134. Later he added, "Such a claim is an arrogant elevation of self to the status of God" (ibid., 137).

37. Timothy Ashley, *The Book of Numbers*, NICOT, 295.

38. Craigie, *Deuteronomy*, 187. Eugene Merrill has demonstrated that remembering was an essential part of the nation's worship. In Israel, he pointed out, there was an

Second, we must remember the Old Testament emphasis on human aggression and non-neutrality. To forget the LORD was "to go after other gods and serve them and worship them" (Deut. 8:19; cf. 4:15–31). Worshipful remembrance in trusting God would mean life, but idolatry "like the nations" would mean death "because you would not obey the voice of the LORD your God" (8:20). Idolatry is not necessarily gross or repulsive; however, it is always ungodly in its preference for dead idols over the living God. For Israel, idolatry was nothing less than a breach in national character and a denial of the heart of its faith (cf. 6:5, 16).

The Foundational Conflict between God and Self

Moses' warnings transfer without tarnish from ancient Israel to contemporary situations, perhaps because the issue is who we are in light of the biblical God. Is he the living Standard of our behavior, or is he an abstract speculation who can conform to our social ideals and expectations? We are taught from our infancy to strive for significance and success. The goal and prize is a parade of accomplishments, with appropriate status symbols for all to see the fruits of our ambition and the might of our hands. I remember vividly a Christian conference that my wife and I attended in my spiritual infancy. At the gathering people would share their interests, hobbies, and position in life. Soon I was caught up in the need to impress people around me with their good fortune at having me in attendance. If the topic was sports, I could rattle off my victories. If the topic was expertise, I could exhibit an indelible memory of what I knew. If the topic was recognitions, then I could point to an impressive array of promotions and awards. Of course, none of these claims was as large as I made them. In my mind, I was reflecting the ways of

inextricable connection between worship and daily activities. "Remembering: A Central Theme in Biblical Worship," *JETS* 43, 1 (March 2000): 27–36.

the "real world," where this sort of pride was expected. Do not the fittest survive and succeed? If we expect to win, should we not have confidence that we are better than other people?

Before long one of the leaders took me aside and asked, "Whom are you trying to impress?" He explained that I was turning people off. If I had accomplished anything, he advised, then the Lord had given it to me. I was taken aback and deeply offended by the well-meaning counsel. He had hit me at the foundation of my self-esteem and self-perceived significance. He was the first one to deliver the sermon that I most needed to hear.

Forty years later, I laugh about my wounded ego. I laugh at the pretentiousness of my trumped-up claims. I laugh at the way that I nurtured the wrong hormones. No one doubts that pride is the way that the sinful world operates. But I now rejoice that God has taught me the wisdom of his Word as expressed by the godly leader. Of course, success and wealth are not sinful in themselves, because it is God "who gives you power to get wealth" (Deut. 8:18). Instead, they are outward symbols of our inward motives and attitudes in their pursuit. I can identify with Moses' warning to the Israelites, because such behavior is an idolatry of the self that undermines our life with the Lord's people. I realize that God made me with the purpose of living significantly, and he wants me to transfer my ambitions to his service. I have learned that my weakness is his strength. This is what Paul meant in 2 Corinthians 12:9: "But he said to me, 'My grace is sufficient for you, for my power is made perfect in weakness.'" The memory of God's mighty acts in saving me from myself cause me to be grateful for his grace rather than adversarial toward potential competitors for vainglory. I still dislike and resist the truth, just as I do not want to be reminded that I will die someday. But my denials do not change the facts of life. Pride is a deadly vice!

We have seen that the Pentateuch consistently affirms that the conflict between pride and humility is central to life on earth.

God's creation of humanity began with a command. Humility is an attitude of obedience and a conviction that trusting the Lord for his provisions is the pathway of life. We may not have everything we want, but we will have what we need (cf. Deut. 8:4). Pride, conversely, is the rebellious attitude of disobedience that seeks personal significance independently from God. Pride attributes successes to one's own abilities with no thought of the enabling presence of God. Of course, this approach is natural for an unbelieving world with no perceivable allegiance to the sovereign Creator; life is nasty and short, and may the best person win because this existence is the only one that has evolved. Many of us are adrift in a sea of endless attempts to play God without creaturely limitations. The end of such attempts, many people hope, is an ideal world of peace and happiness instead of the unbroken chain of wars that have characterized history. In contrast, we as believers are to live each day in worshipful remembrance of God's saving goodness in our lives as opposed to an idolatrous forgetfulness that dismisses him from daily labors. The consequence of the choice is life or death. The will to power at Babel was matched by Israel's self-glorification in the land. Both generations were scattered and perished in exile.

On the basis of the Pentateuchal narratives, we will now turn to biblical wisdom, where we find that God's commandments are lamps and His teachings are lights in "the way of life" (Prov. 6:23). The reverse is that "there is a way that seems right to a man, but its end is the way to death" (14:12). Wisdom develops the biblical storyline poetically by expanding a simple truth: God opposes the proud and exalts the humble.

Summary

From the beginning of human history, pride (self-centeredness) and humility (God-centeredness) are opposing responses to God's will for the earth. Foundationally, sin is pride, which is rebellion against God. Abram exemplified humility by trusting God for his needs and divine promises for his future. Moses is the model for humility in his aggressive leadership of Israel for God's glory.

Key Terms

antithetical. Opposite.

city. In the Bible, the organized gathering of unbelievers to find security apart from God.

covenant. An arrangement for relationship between God and humanity, initiated by God.

depravity. The universal condition of sinful humanity.

face. An Old Testament metaphor for presence, as in Moses' face-to-face encounters with God.

God-centeredness. A concern for submission to God in all of life's circumstances, or "lov[ing] the Lord your God with all your heart and with all your soul and with all your mind" (Matt. 22:37).

idol. An object of worship other than the Trinitarian God.

image. A representation of a person that suggests their character.

imago Dei. The essential significance of a human person as created by God, supremely of the incarnate Jesus Christ.

labyrinth. A metaphor for the complexity of life that obscures God-pleasing living.

paradigm. A model of how something or someone should be understood.

Pentateuch. The first five books of the Bible, the books of Moses, the Torah.

prescient. Foresight of actions or events before they occur.

revelation. Knowledge given by God.

self-centeredness. More than selfishness, the prioritizing of self in the circumstances of life, a self-sufficiency in living with no regard for God.

sin. An act or condition of breaking divine law, especially religious as distinct from evil.

walk. A biblical metaphor for faithful dependence on God in daily details.

Questions for Discussion

1. How did Satan tempt Adam and Eve? Is this the paradigm for our temptations?

2. Can we have a biblical understanding of sin and righteousness without a prior understanding of God?

3. How does Abram's pilgrimage by faith illustrate a godly walk?

4. After humanity's fall into sin, does the divinely bestowed *imago Dei* continue? If all people retain this image, how can we explain the importance of faith for a full expression of the image?

5. Does the Bible ever give a detailed definition or description of humility and pride? How does it communicate the importance of these character traits?

6. In Deuteronomy 8, did God predict that Israel would be characterized by humility as his people?

7. How do the emphases of the Pentateuch give us wisdom for living today?

8. Why is a humble commitment to God always limited to a remnant of believers?

9. How does Miriam's leprosy illustrate God's humiliation of pride?

10. How did Jesus, when he was tempted in the wilderness, illustrate God's exaltation of humility?

For Further Reading

Smith, David L. *With Willful Intent: A Theology of Sin.* Wheaton, IL: Bridgepoint, 1994. Most of the literature focuses on pride under the heading of "sin," which speaks volumes about the neglect of humility. Smith surveys historical, biblical, systematic, and practical dimensions of sin with noteworthy references to various nuances of pride.

3

The Humiliation of Pride in the Wisdom Literature

MARTIN LUTHER, the famous Protestant Reformer, became professor of biblical theology at Wittenberg at the age of twenty-nine. Among his first lectures were his expositions of the Psalms. These studies initiated his conviction that obedience is the humility that breaks through humanity's resistance to the Word of God. The outward barrier was the depravity of the world that trapped sinners in its vortex. For Luther, humility meant agreement with God that all people are sinners in need of justification by faith, which is a gateway to forgiveness and freedom from the world's bondage. Our admission that God is right is the "obedience of faith."

Luther's obedience in trusting God for salvation led to the humility of trusting God as his fortress through constant conflicts with Catholicism, many of his countrymen, and fellow Protestants. As an unbroken chain of conflicts swirled around him, Luther suffered bouts of depression in which his faith found refuge in the certainties of God and his Word. In a year of deep despondency (1527), he found encouragement in Psalm 46 and wrote "A mighty fortress is our God, a bulwark never failing." With Job he would sing, "For still our ancient foe doth seek to work us woe." With the sons of Korah he would sing, "The LORD of hosts is with us; the God of Jacob is our fortress" (Ps. 46:7; cf. v. 11). With the authors of the Proverbs he rested knowing that "He must win the battle amid the flood of mortal ills prevailing." We will discover with Luther that humility is an essential foundation for Christian living, not merely as a rest from spiritual conflicts but also as a basis of hope to persevere in our walk with the Lord.

Wisdom Literature in the Old Testament consists of a group of books that are found between their historical and prophetic neighbors. They usually include Job, Psalms, Proverbs, Ecclesiastes, and the Song of Solomon. The first three books have much to say about the ways of humanity and God on the world's stage. The world languishes in the grip of pride, which is self-centeredness that leads to self-destruction: "There is a way that seems right to a man, but its end is the way to death" (Prov. 14:12). A humble person acknowledges personal limitations and seeks the strength of the Lord in the circumstances of life: "The Lord of hosts is with us; the God of Jacob is our fortress" (Ps. 46:7).

We will explore Old Testament wisdom with three antitheses—opposites that draw the line between pride and humility:

1. Job: popular wisdom versus godly humility
2. Psalms: ungodly pride versus humble faith
3. Proverbs: humiliation of pride versus exaltation of humility

Job presented Satan as the adversary of creation, who accused God of a manipulative relationship with his people. Faith is a fraud, Satan argued, because covenantal relationship is for mutual advantage rather than creaturely dependence on the grace of the Creator. Job learned that popular notions about suffering are the real charade. Humanity's limitations are so great that they can only trust God's sufficiency through the mazes of life. The Psalms are concerned with arrogant adversaries of God and believers. In humble faith godly people are to find refuge in the Lord, knowing that he will hear their prayers and bless them according to Proverbs.

Job: Popular Wisdom versus Godly Humility

Job describes a righteous man, who endured agonizing suffering with exemplary perseverance (James 5:11). He was "blameless and upright, one who feared God and turned away from evil" (Job 1:1). Most scholars think that the book's setting is the second millennium B.C., perhaps in proximity to Abraham. It is a pastoral guide for hurting saints, which seeks to reconcile God's power and goodness with unbearably painful circumstances. If he is able to remove suffering, why doesn't he do it? The book counsels an acceptance of God's character, even if his will and purpose cannot be fully understood or explained. Traditional answers, according to Job, failed to comfort righteous sufferers. They appealed to an easy logic that attributed intense pain to sinful causes. But what if the sinful causes are unknown? Humility and pride are undertones in that the former is faithful acceptance of circumstances under God, while pride is rebellion against God for injustices in life. This point emerges in the use of the terms and the way that Job's friends explain suffering.

With a glance back at creation, the book of Job presents Satan, the adversary in Eden, as tempter once again in the presence of God's heavenly court. Instead of Adam and Eve, he now seeks to destroy creation by trying to alienate a godly patriarch. Job appears as a person in God's image who sought understanding about his relationship with the Creator. In other words, Job was a covenantal creature who was selected to test the validity of God's will for his creation. When God commended his servant Job as a uniquely righteous man, who "fears God and turns away from evil" (Job 1:8), Satan charged that his faith in God was a sham. Job, he claimed, was self-serving; he was righteous because it was advantageous for his prosperity.

This temptation was aimed at the heart of the relationship between God and humanity. If correct, the godliness of righteous people would be a manipulative exercise based on merit. The structure of creation would be flawed to the extent that it would have to be judged out of existence because of the unrighteousness of humanity's best efforts. In other words, if the link between righteousness and blessing could be broken, then the covenantal relationship would be exposed as fraud, a mere cover for mutual advantage rather than the truth of creaturely dependence on God for life itself. An important lesson in Job is that one of our greatest temptations is to love our gifts rather than their Giver. We are tempted to please God merely for the sake of his benefits: "But stretch out your hand and touch all that he has, and he will curse you to your face" (Job 1:11). Once raised, the accusation could not be ignored or silenced, for the unanswered accusation would be an admission of the flaw.

So God let Satan have his way with Job, short of taking his life, to vindicate his creation (Job 1:12). The test became Job's season of agony, deprived as he was of every sign of God's favor. His loss was catastrophic: seven thousand sheep, three thousand camels, five hundred oxen and donkeys, numerous servants, seven sons and three daughters, and his health. Through unimaginable tragedies, the great man was reduced to life without any benefits. Furthermore, he suffered alone without understanding, knowing within himself that his faith was authentic and that he would see his Redeemer in the end (19:25–26). He could curse the day of his birth and chide God for perceived injustices, but he refused to repudiate his Maker as his wife had proposed (2:9).

Beyond his apparent loss of divine favor, Job was hounded by the popular thinking of his friends. They confidently assumed that a traditional consensus and abstract reasoning could explain all of God's ways in everyone's circumstances. In a cameo of this kind of thinking, Jesus' disciples inquired about the man born blind. "Rabbi, who sinned, this man or his parents, that he was born blind?" (John 9:2). That is, suffering is punishment for sin, so who is the guilty party? However, mirroring Job's message, Jesus answered, "It was not that this man sinned, or his parents, but that the works of God might be displayed in him" (v. 3). When questioned by the authorities, the healed man could simply say, "He put mud on my eyes, and I washed, and I see" (v. 15; cf. vv. 11, 25). Job too was at a loss for words, and both men were outcasts in their societies (cf. vv. 34–35). In anguish and anger, Job clearly grasped that popular wisdom failed to comprehend his situation.

The sin that Job's friends had in mind was pride. Bildad the Shuhite reasoned that God could not be unjust, so Job's circumstances proved that he and his family must have been sinful (Job 8:3–4). If Job would "plead with the Almighty" in uprightness, then "he will . . . restore your rightful habitation" (vv. 5–6). Elihu was more explicit. Job's cries to the Lord, he believed, were arrogant:

> Because of the multitude of oppressions people cry out;
>   they call for help because of the arm of the mighty.
> But none says, "Where is God my Maker,
>   who gives songs in the night . . . ?"
> There they cry out, but he does not answer,
>   because of the pride of evil men.
> Surely God does not hear an empty cry,
>   nor does the Almighty regard it. (35:9–10, 12–13)

Elihu's emphasis was that God does not respond to the cries of oppressed people who arrogantly disregard God their Maker.[1] Therefore, Job must be one of them. In chapter 36 Elihu offered the circumstantial argument positively as well: "He does not withdraw his eyes from the righteous, but with kings on the throne he sets them forever, and they are exalted" (v. 7). That is, exalted people like kings must be righteous because of their privileged lives. A negative proposal follows, "And if they are bound in chains and caught in the cords of affliction, then he declares to them their work and their transgressions, that they are behaving arrogantly" (36:8–9).[2] The afflicted, in Elihu's opinion, must accept the evident justice of God and not complain about their suffering.

Without any awareness of the heavenly confrontation between God and Satan, Job earnestly sought an explanation about why God had allowed him, a righteous follower, to endure such agonizing suffering. Job passed the tests of his faith in deprivation and ignorance by subjecting himself to divine wisdom without stalking godlessly into the dark night of his condition. Everyone was silenced but God, who revealed to Job the inscrutable ways of the Almighty (Job 38:1–41:34). We must keep in mind that we knew about the heavenly confrontation at the beginning, as well as the restorations at the end. Job did not, and his lack of knowledge was a large part of his bewilderment. He demanded true

---

1. "Elihu felt that failure of suffering men to see their Maker is also the author of wisdom and joy is a sign of arrogance on their part. . . . Job might not be wicked, but he shared this arrogance and so got no answer (v. 14)." Elmer Smick, *Job*, ed. Frank E. Gaebelein et al., EBC 4 (Grand Rapids: Zondervan, 1988), 1016–17 We should note that if pride is self-centered disregard of God, then Job's cries, in fact, would be a humble response.

2. "The fundamental thought of Elihu here once again comes unmistakably to view: the sufferings of the righteous are well-meant chastisements, which are to wean them from the sins into which through carnal security they have fallen—a warning from God to penitence, designed to work their good." F. Delitzsch, *Biblical Commentary on the Book of Job*, 2 vols., trans. Francis Bolton (Grand Rapids: Eerdmans, 1949), 2:279.

wisdom, and the author of the book inserts a poetic argument that ultimate wisdom can be found only in God (28:20–27). People can understand a great deal about creaturely matters, but they cannot know God's ways. For them "the fear of the Lord, that is wisdom, and to turn away from evil is understanding" (v. 28).[3] The summarizing statement—a hinge of the book—stands at the juncture between Job's character (1:8), his friends' sterile advice, and Job's appeal (chaps. 29–31) with God's vindication.

God's response to Job's appeal was an eloquent tour of his creation, interestingly with more questions than answers. He pointed to the earth's foundation, the boundaries of water and light, the heavenly orders, and the plentitude of creatures. He did not reveal his grand design or explain the satanic challenge. Instead, he revealed himself, and his presence satisfied Job: "I have uttered what I did not understand, things too wonderful for me, which I did not know. . . . therefore, I despise myself and repent in dust and ashes" (Job 42:3, 6). We must notice that the presence of the Lord provoked this response rather than any argument or human answer. Job confessed that he had been complaining about things that he could not understand. As hard as this is for us to contemplate, Job would have done better to pray reverently in the midst of his agonies. His message is that suffering saints do not know the battles behind the scenes, and they can embrace their circumstances only in the perspective of God's incomparable Reality. God is the answer! The message is reinforced by God's revelation of humility as the acceptance of divine provision for human needs. The Lord's displeasure with Job's friends was reconciled by their sacrifices and Job's prayer for them: "And the Lord restored the fortunes of Job, when he had prayed for his friends" (42:10).

3. Job's summary is akin to Ecclesiastes 12:13: "The end of the matter; all has been heard. Fear God and keep his commandments, for this is the whole duty of man" (cf. Prov. 1:7).

An interesting part of the LORD's challenge concerns the inability of people to govern God's world. They cannot clothe themselves with divine splendor, and

> Look on everyone who is proud and bring him low
>   and tread down the wicked where they stand.
> Hide them all in the dust together;
>   bind their faces in the world below.
> Then will I also acknowledge to you
>   that your own right hand can save you. (40:12–14)

The pride of wicked people is so deeply ingrained in the sinful human condition that only God's grace can save them. The LORD indirectly affirms that unbelief is pride and that godlessness leads to death and a destiny "in the world below." Usually people are caught up in the injustices of their own circumstances, but they cannot imagine the magnitude of pride in the world and consign its wicked representatives to eternal punishment. The indictment points to the extent and depth of arrogant unbelief in fallen humanity.[4] Only the LORD can be fully aware of such things, and only he can save people of faith from their suffering and bring them to his presence eternally.

God was present in the depths with Job, even as he was pointing forward to his own Son, the Lord Jesus, who suffered terrible injustices and death to vindicate God's covenant with mankind. But Jesus did not come for the gifts; he came "not to be served but to serve, and to give his life as a ransom for many" (Mark 10:45). He differed from Job in his knowledge of his mission, but that only magnified his cry, "My God, my God, why have you forsaken me?" (15:34). The cross framed Jesus' humble obedience, his body

4. "God stated that wickedness exists and that he alone had the power to uphold his own honor by crushing it. Deliverance from all evil rests with God, not with man (vv. 9–14)." Smick, *Job*, 1048.

scarred by Job-like afflictions that exposed the arrogance of our violent world in conflict with the greater love of God. Obedience is submission to the will of God rather than self-assertion against God. Therefore, even as Job was doubly blessed, Paul writes of Jesus that "God has highly exalted him and bestowed on him the name that is above every name, so that at the name of Jesus every knee should bow, in heaven and on earth and under the earth, and every tongue confess that Jesus Christ is Lord, to the glory of God the Father" (Phil. 2:9–11). Humility in Job is submission to God's wisdom, even in the most adverse circumstances, knowing that in the end, God will exalt his humble servants. In God's future, popular wisdom about prosperity will be replaced by godly wisdom about fearing God and turning from the evils of pride (cf. Job 28:28).

Psalms: Ungodly Pride versus Humble Faith

The Psalms continue Job's theme of humility as obedience to God in spite of adverse circumstances. However, two differences distinguish Psalms and Proverbs from Job. First, the focus shifts from Satan as an unseen adversary to wicked adversaries on earth, who rebel against God and oppress his faithful followers. Second, the friends' prevailing perspective that suffering indicates arrogance before God is shifted to the oppression by ungodly adversaries, even though there are Job-like glimmers of humility in texts like Psalm 131:1–2: "O LORD, my heart is not lifted up; my eyes are not raised too high; I do not occupy myself with things too great and too marvelous for me." People suffered not because they were tested in their prosperity but because arrogant sinners persecuted them. If Job was characterized by a concept of humility as reverential perseverance, then the Psalms use the concept similarly with reference to believers who find refuge in the Lord.

Psalms and Proverbs divide people into two types, the wicked (רֶשַׁע) and the righteous (צַדִּיק), who are opposed in their attitudes and behavior (cf. Prov. 10). Three subjects are in view: righteous believers, wicked adversaries, and the Lord. With this in mind, "ungodly" or "godly" behavior would be appropriate equivalents. We should not assume that godly is synonymous with God's people. Ungodly Israelites' oppression of their unfortunate countrymen sometimes was too pervasive to allow for such a clear division.

The context for the labels was covenantal relationship, so that *righteousness* described those who trusted God and were just in their treatment of other people. Again, we are reminded that the biblical meanings of humility and pride necessitate God as the matrix of our understanding. However, we should not speak, as we do now, of merely good and bad people socially—as valid as that distinction might be. We must consider how our thinking about God affects our treatment of people. Also, justice is central to the biblical distinction, and the wicked are frequently contrasted with their poor and afflicted victims. The Bible affirms that many wealthy people were wicked because they oppressed vulnerable members of their society to gain their wealth. By the same token, many poor Israelites were impoverished because they refused to follow wicked practices to gain wealth.

The wicked versus righteous distinction corresponded to arrogant versus humble behavior, with respect to the Lord. The psalmists, particularly David, wrote in humility and faith. There are many types of psalms, but we are concerned with the laments, in which believers cried out to God for deliverance from their godless persecutors. As noted earlier, the humble (עָנָו) experienced God as their hope and deliverer, a refuge in their suffering.[5]

5. The primary terms are עָנָו ("humble") or עֲנָוָה ("humility") and עָנִי ("poor, afflicted") or עֳנִי, אֳנִי ("poverty, affliction"). Wolfgang Bauder concludes: "Hence

Kidner relates them to "'the poor' in the first beatitude, as being those who are in need and know it."[6] Like Moses in Numbers 12:3, they "walk in the law of the LORD . . . keep his testimonies, . . . seek him with their whole heart, . . . walk in his ways" (Ps. 119:1–3; cf. vv. 174–75). Sometimes this devotion came from their circumstances: "Before I was afflicted I went astray, but now I keep your word" (v. 67; cf. v. 176). They viewed the treacherous hatred of their enemies as an opportunity to experience guidance from the Lord: "He leads the humble in what is right, and teaches the humble his way" (25:9; cf. vv. 2–3, 16–19; 5:8). Though admittedly strangers on earth for their devotion to God's word, their souls longed for his commands, because "you rebuke the insolent, accursed ones, who wander from your commandments" (119:21). Because adversaries were numerous, the psalmists plead for deliverance from them: "Plead my cause and redeem me; give me life according to your promise!" (v. 154). This emphasis is the same one seen up to this point; humility is trusting God regardless of circumstances.

The Psalms provide a detailed sketch of the prideful persecutors. Generally, they were viewed as personally wealthy, socially influential, and seemingly exempt from suffering:

> For I was envious of the arrogant
> when I saw the prosperity of the wicked.

'anî and particularly 'anaw change their meaning from those who are materially poor, and become the self-chosen religious title of those who are in deep need and difficulty, humbly seek help from Yahweh alone, or have found it there." *NIDNTT*, s.v. "Humility," by Hans-Helmut Esser, 2:257. Walther Eichrodt similarly states: "Here *the relationship of earthly goods* could find expression in the use of 'aniqqim, 'poor' or 'wretched' as a title of honour for the pious, interpreted by the parallel term 'enawim, 'meek,' meaning those who persevere in a right attitude of humility toward God as well as toward men, and who are therefore assured of the divine good pleasure and salvation." *Theology of the Old Testament*, 2 vols., trans. J. A. Baker (Philadelphia: Westminster, 1967), 2:360.

6. Derek Kidner, *Psalms 1–72*, 2 vols., TOTC, 1:94.

For they have no pangs until death;
 their bodies are fat and sleek.
They are not in trouble as others are;
 they are not stricken like the rest of mankind. . . .
Behold, these are the wicked;
 always at ease, they increase in riches. (73:3–5, 12; cf.
  10:5–6)

Their wealth and influence attracted fawning followers, "Therefore his people turn back to them, and find no fault in them" (73:10).[7] Their increase in wrongful riches compounded their arrogance and self-sufficiency (62:10; 140:8). Their pride in status sustained itself by dismissing accountability toward God and by unceasing oppression of weaker people:

Therefore pride is their necklace;
 violence covers them as a garment. . . .
They scoff and speak with malice;
 loftily they threaten oppression. . . .
And they say, "How can God know?
 Is there knowledge in the Most High?" (73:6, 8, 11)

This dismissal of God was their most evident difference from humble believers. Psalm 10 is a forceful indictment of their wicked rejection of God:

In the pride of his face the wicked does not seek him;
 all his thoughts are, "There is no God." . . .
He says in his heart, "God has forgotten,
 he has hidden his face, he will never see it." . . .

---

7. "The Hebrew emendations are fairly small, and most modern versions find here the popular worship of success." Derek Kidner, *Psalms 73–150*, TOTC, 2:261.

> Why does the wicked renounce God
> and say in his heart, "You will not call to account"? (vv. 4,
> 11, 13)[8]

David presented a portrait of a godless man: materialistic, uncaring toward his fellows, and thoroughly calloused in the cravings of his heart. His arrogance was so addictive that he rejoiced in his godlessness. In Kidner's words, "It is the arrogance of this man, adding Godward insult to manward injury, that dominates this account of him."[9]

The godless man's rebellious attitude toward authority, both God and king, was reflected in their attitude, their speech, and their outward demeanor. His heart was calloused, in contrast to the psalmist, who kept "with my whole heart . . . your precepts" (Ps. 119:69). Similarly, in 17:10 David states, "They close their hearts to pity; with their mouths they speak arrogantly." The weapon of the evil heart is the tongue: "His mouth is filled with cursing and deceit and oppression; under his tongue are mischief and iniquity" (10:7; cf. 5:9). In the same vein, "For the sin of their mouths, the words of their lips, let them be trapped in their pride" (59:12; cf. 94:4).

The connection between the heart and its expression through speech places pride at the core of oppressors' corrupt character. Wolff states, "The supreme importance of the ear and of speech for true human understanding is unmistakable."[10] Unbelief is a willful rejection of God and his people, an uplifted glorification of self, which is pride. The problem is compounded

---

8. The psalm is connected to the preceding one by the Greek translation of the Old Testament and the Vulgate. The absence of a title in Psalm 10 and the continuation of an acrostic style support the connection. Together they teach the triumph of God on behalf of his people (Ps. 9) in spite of the present dominance of evil (Ps. 10).

9. Kidner, *Psalms 1–72*, 1:71.

10. Hans Walter Wolff, *Anthropology of the Old Testament*, trans. Margaret Kohl (Philadelphia: Fortress, 1974), 75.

since the adversaries often were familiar with God and his Word, but they openly rejected godly options in favor of their own advantage. The allegiance of the heart comes first, then body language follows.

While the eyes of the humble are "ever toward the Lord," uplifted and lightened in hope (Ps. 25:15; cf. 141:8), the eyes of the proud are haughty (18:27). Haughty eyes are "the lamp" of the wicked and reflect the proud heart (Prov. 21:4). They are portrayed as wild predators, which "stealthily watch for the helpless" (Ps. 10:8). They stalk, trap, and drag their victims away to be devoured. And wicked oppressors "freely strut about, when what is vile is honored among men" (12:8, NIV).

From the contrast of humility and pride we can draw important conclusions about the relationship between God, proud rebels, and humble believers. The reader may imagine these three characters as the points of a triangle. The proud aggressors ignored God and attacked vulnerable people for self-centered gain, including the king if expedient. Their attacks were usually verbal. We have seen from Psalms 5, 10, and 73 that their litany of sins included lies and false accusations, slander, threats, curses, mocking, taunting, and contempt (cf. 31:18; 35:11; 119:23, 51).

In Job we witnessed well-meaning but misdirected advice. Here we are dealing with mean-spirited thugs. Sometimes their persecutions became physically threatening with violent behavior (cf. 86:14; 119:122; 140:4–5). VanGemeren observes this violence in Psalm 5, "The 'bloodthirsty' man is, therefore, not necessarily one who is guilty of murder, but one who no longer knows the limits between 'mine' and 'thine' and thus twists and perverts justice, even at the cost of human lives or dignity (cf. Isa. 3:13–15; 5:8–10; Amos 6:12)."[11] With malice toward God, they lived according to their own rules.

11. Willem VanGemeren, *Psalms*, ed. Frank Gaebelein et al, EBC 5 (Grand Rapids: Zondervan, 1991), 89.

Humble believers, on the other hand, were not to retaliate. Our impulse is to respond in kind and to intimidate our opponents to the extent that they will leave us alone. Instead the Psalms counsel believers to aggressively seek the Lord's vengeance on their enemies. However, their prayers and righteous behavior were neither passive neutrality nor a retreat. With confidence they sought the Lord's intervention in their behalf, and their God-centeredness nuanced the meaning of biblical humility. This is evidenced in examples of self-humiliation as a testimony, even in the face of their adversaries (cf. Ps. 35:11–16).

This humble trust in God in a hostile setting is part of a biblical principle: God will bring accountability and judgment on arrogant behavior. Moses sang prophetically to his generation, "Vengeance is mine, and recompense, . . . I will take vengeance on my adversaries and will repay those who hate me" (Deut. 32:35, 41). Paul quoted Moses in Romans 12:19: "Beloved, never avenge yourselves, but leave it to the wrath of God, for it is written, 'Vengeance is mine, I will repay, says the Lord.'"

The principle of divine justice arose from three truths in the Psalms, which believers were to apply as they maintained their righteous behavior. First, they lived with an unwavering conviction about the Lord's hatred of pride. With no equivocation David proclaimed in Psalm 5:4–5:

> For you are not a God who delights in wickedness;
> > evil may not dwell with you,
> The boastful shall not stand before your eyes;
> > you hate all evildoers.[12]

---

12. Proverbs 6:16–17 lists haughty eyes, a lying tongue, and a wicked heart among seven things that the Lord hates. 21:4 affirms, "Haughty eyes and a proud heart, the lamp of the wicked, are sin."

Therefore, "you save a humble people," David continued, "but the haughty eyes you bring down" (18:27; cf. 2 Sam. 22:28). As king, he resolved to follow the Lord's direction:

> Whoever slanders his neighbor secretly
> > I will destroy.
> Whoever has a haughty look and an arrogant heart
> > I will not endure. (101:5)

One can assume that God would honor the prayers of a king after his own heart. Beyond individual prayers, a community lament called for God's vengeance on the arrogance of the wicked in accord with the nonretaliatory approach noted above:

> Rise up, O judge of the earth;
> > repay to the proud what they deserve!
> O LORD, how long shall the wicked,
> > how long shall the wicked exult?
> They pour out their arrogant words;
> > all the evildoers boast. (94:2–4)

In VanGemeren's words, "The just Judge cannot tolerate 'the proud' (*ge'îm*), who act autonomously without regard for God, his people, or the orderly rule of God. . . . he will bring them what they 'deserve' (*g-m-l*; cf. 28:4; Lam. 3:64)."[13] We must note the passion with which the Lord, the king, and faithful believers expressed their opposition to the proud. In spite of pressure from adversaries, David and faithful Israelites knew that true security rested in God alone: "Blessed is the man who makes the LORD his trust, who does not turn to the proud, to those who go astray after a lie!" (40:4).

13. VanGemeren, *Psalms*, 610–11.

These expressions reflect a cluster of images that describe the "aggression" of humble believers against arrogance—a proactive stance that we are not inclined to notice at first glance. Rather than seeking vengeance, they prayed to God as their refuge and maintained a life of dependence on the Lord, who was their inexhaustible source of strength in times of persecution. "Refuge," Luther's image in his "A Mighty Fortress," occurs nearly fifty times in the Psalms and suggests a fortress, or a stronghold, which gave believers safety and security as they withstood their adversaries (cf. Ps. 144:2). God as "fortress" is also used with images of him like "rock" (foundational stability) and shield (protection). The images are clustered in Moses' prophetic song in Deuteronomy 32. David also gathers them in his praise for deliverance from his enemies:

> I love you, O Lord, my strength.
> The Lord is my rock and my fortress and my deliverer,
>> my God, my rock, in whom I take refuge,
>> my shield, and the horn of my salvation, my stronghold.
> I call upon the Lord, who is worthy to be praised,
>> and I am saved from my enemies. (18:1–3; cf. 2 Sam. 22:2–4)

Second, believers projected their experience of God's goodness and his hatred of pride to his promise that the humble would inherit the promised land of blessing. With assurance from God's Word, godly people hoped for a time when things would be rectified. Accordingly, David counseled trust in God's judgment on evildoers:

> Fret not yourself because of evildoers; . . .
>> Trust in the Lord, and do good; . . .
> In just a little while, the wicked will be no more;
>> though you look carefully at his place, he will not be there.

But the meek shall inherit the land
    and delight themselves in abundant peace,
The wicked plots against the righteous
    and gnashes his teeth at him,
but the Lord laughs at the wicked,
    for he sees that his day is coming. (Ps. 37:1, 3, 10–13)

This is a psalm about ultimate outcomes, and Old Testament wisdom recognized that God might wait until a distant future to fully display the different destinies of the humble and the proud. This assurance reemerges in prophets like Zephaniah, who proclaimed to Israel:

On that day you shall not be put to shame
    because of the deeds by which you have rebelled against me;
for then I will remove from your midst
    your proudly exultant ones,
and you shall no longer be haughty
    in my holy mountain.
But I will leave in your midst
    a people humble and lowly.
They shall seek refuge in the name of the LORD. (Zeph. 3:11–12)

In the prophet's setting, "proudly exultant ones" were complacent, self-indulgent people who contemptuously ignored God in his holy mountain (1:8–13).[14]

Third, along with ultimate outcomes, humble believers experienced the goodness of the Lord in answer to their prayers. In the midst of their individual laments, the psalmists changed

---

14. Jesus used Psalm 37:11 in his third beatitude, "Blessed are the meek, for they shall inherit the earth" (Matt. 5:5). The way of wisdom, he taught, is to trust in God's direction in life's circumstances rather than self-assertion to further one's public prestige, especially at the expense of other people.

from despair to praise for the living God's intervention on their behalf. The change is reflected both in the grammar (the *waw* adversative) and in the content of the verses. In Claus Westermann's words,

> The transition within the prayer which is indicated by the clauses with *but* occurs uniquely in the Psalms of Israel. In them there is the strongest witness to the reality of the help that is experienced, the condescending of God to the one who cries out to him.[15]

Allender and Longman point to the same reality in the psalmists' encounters with God in their suffering:

> This is the central message of the book of Psalms: *we encounter divine goodness in the midst of pain.* . . . The psalms provide no formula for the bridge from lament to joy—no steps to healing, no principles to practice. God does not tolerate manipulation of truth to escape from struggle. He longs for faith that struggles and rests in his goodness.[16]

The transition may not have removed the problem, but the encounter was an assurance of the presence of the Lord, who would avenge their pain. Ultimately, the believer knew that God's presence would bring deliverance from their pain (cf. Josh. 23:10).[17]

Westermann's remarkable observation about the unique transitions in Israel's psalms points to an even deeper reality of godly faith. In the strength of the Lord, the poor, persecuted

---

15. Claus Westermann, *The Praise of God in the Psalms*, trans. Keith Crim (Richmond: John Knox, 1965), 73.

16. Dan Allender and Tremper Longman III, *The Cry of the Soul: How Our Emotions Reveal Our Deepest Questions about God* (Colorado Springs: NavPress, 1994), 245, 247.

17. VanGemeren provides an excellent summary of "Yahweh Is My Redeemer," in his *Psalms*, 763–68.

believers were not weak. Dependence on the Lord opened them to God's irresistible strength and his victory over arrogant adversaries. The emphasis pervades Scripture and will reemerge in the chapters on the Gospels and Epistles. A humble attitude allows the power of God to work through us in place of our own insufficient efforts. In him they cease to be impotent victims and could courageously pursue their countercultural godliness:

> Love the LORD, all you his saints!
> The LORD preserves the faithful
>> but abundantly repays the one who acts in pride.
> Be strong, and let your heart take courage,
>> all you who wait on the LORD! (Ps. 31:23–24)

Hence, they boast, but their pride is in the Lord rather than themselves:

> Through you we push down our foes;
>> through your name we tread down those who rise up
>>> against us.
> For not in my bow do I trust,
>> nor can my sword save me.
> But you have saved us from our foes
>> and have put to shame those who hate us.
> In God we have boasted continually,
>> and we will give thanks to your name forever. (44:5–8)

This is the legitimate side of pride in the Bible.

The titles of the Psalms point to the Davidic narratives in the books of Samuel and Chronicles as an illustration of their teaching on humility: Absalom (Ps. 3), Saul and various enemies (Pss. 18, 52, 54, 57, 59, 142), Abimelech (Ps. 34), Nathan's confrontation (Ps. 51), the Philistines (Ps. 56), as well as Aram Naharain/Aram and Zobah/Edomites (Ps. 60). They take us initially to the Israelites' demand for "a king . . . like all the nations," which was displeasing to Samuel and a rejection of God's kingship (1 Sam. 8:1–9; 10:19). Samuel warned the people about the oppressive policies of a king modeled by other nations (8:10–22). The prophet was directed to Saul, a son of Kish, who was "a handsome young man. There was not a man among the people of Israel more handsome than he. From his shoulders upward, he was taller than any of the people" (9:1–2; 10:23–24). The Israelites wanted an intimidating hero rather than a man of God. They wanted to be proud of their leader and shouted, "Long live the king!" (10:24). But God rejected Saul for disobedience (chaps. 13–15), a king who reflected the character of the people.

The LORD then instructed Samuel to find a different king among the sons of Jesse the Bethlehemite (1 Sam. 16:1–3). The criterion was neither formidable appearance nor intimidating height, because "the LORD sees not as man sees: man looks on the outward appearance, but the LORD looks on the heart" (v. 7). After a procession of likely candidates, the LORD selected the youngest son, who was tending the sheep (vv. 11–12; cf. 2 Sam. 5:2; 7:7–8). The Spirit of the LORD "rushed upon David from that day forward" (1 Sam. 13). David, a warrior king, hardly fits our image of humility (16:18), but he harmonizes well with the biblical virtue as exemplified by Moses. He was aggressive for God, while most people in Israel at the time were aggressive for self. Humility, thus defined, makes no sense in a secular setting without God. For example, he faced Goliath "in the name of the LORD of hosts, the God of the armies of Israel" and killed him as with the lion and bear (17:45; cf. v. 36).

Saul feared David because he obviously prospered in the LORD. David, on the other hand, faithfully sought the guidance of the LORD (that is, he "inquired of the LORD") and refused to seek vengeance against God's anointed (e.g., 1 Sam. 24:6–19; 26:5–23; 2 Sam. 9) or his enemies (e.g., 1 Sam. 25:26–33). He even killed those who were swept along by bloodthirsty behavior (e.g., 2 Sam. 3–4). True to the emphasis of biblical humility, David "strengthened himself in the LORD his God," and was "becoming greater and greater, for the LORD, the God of hosts, was with him" (1 Sam. 30:6; 2 Sam. 5:10). Following God's promise of a great name and a perpetual father-son kingship (2 Sam. 7:9–15), David magnified God's incomparable name for his gracious promises to his house (vv. 18–29; cf. Ps. 8).

The turning point for the man after God's heart (Acts 13:22) came when David did not inquire of the LORD and committed adultery with Bathsheba and murdered Uriah (2 Sam. 11). Of course, "the thing that David had done displeased the LORD" (11:27; cf. 12:9–10). The consequences were catastrophic for the king and his family, as he faced rebellion and treachery on every side. David's humility was now expressed as confession in humiliation with "a broken spirit; a broken and contrite heart" (Ps. 51:17). After heartfelt repentance, the prophet Nathan assured him, "The LORD also has put away your sin; you shall not die" (2 Sam. 12:13). Instead David's family and subordinates were shattered by intrigue, culminating in the gruesome death of his son Absalom (chap. 18). Toward the end of his life David reflected on God his rock, fortress, deliverer, and refuge (2 Sam. 22; Ps. 18): "You save a humble people, but your eyes are on the haughty to bring them down" (2 Sam. 22:28). His last recorded words are about the humility of justice:

> When one rules justly over men,
>   ruling in the fear of God,
> he dawns on them like the morning light,
>   like the sun shining forth on a cloudless morning,
>   like rain that makes grass to sprout from the earth. . . .

But worthless men are all like thorns that are thrown away, . . .
and they are utterly consumed with fire. (23:3–4, 6, 7)

David's God-centeredness and repentance after his rebellious behavior is a crucial theme of 2 Chronicles, where God's impending judgment is graciously postponed in light of self-humiliation, as in the cases of Rehoboam, Hezekiah, and Manasseh.[18] Raymond Dillard claims that 2 Chronicles 7:14 is a

> Programmatic statement of great importance. . . . In times of distress or calamity, if the people will humble themselves, pray, and seek God, and turn from wickedness, then God will respond. Each of these terms and their synonyms recur again and again . . . demonstrating that God has indeed kept his promise to Solomon. . . . 'Humbling oneself' (kn') or the failure to do so determines the divine response.[19]

In a noteworthy example, Josiah, king of Judah, read in the scrolls about impending doom for those who had defied the Word of the Lord, and he humbled himself by seeking God's word through the prophetess Huldah. His humility—expressed in his genuine remorse—was honored by the Lord, and judgment was postponed until after his death.

These Davidic narratives shed light on humility and pride in the Wisdom Literature. Their context is theocracy, God's providential governance of his people as their shepherd-king. Arrogant persecutors often were Israelites, and they were rebellious against God like other nations. The hearts of the humble were obedient to the Word of God, and in prayer they sought his protection and guidance. Like David, they were not paralyzed by the threats of their adversaries. Like Noah, Abraham, and

18. Cf. Martin Selman, *2 Chronicles: A Commentary*, TOTC, 515.
19. Raymond Dillard, *2 Chronicles*, WBC 15 (Waco, TX: Word, 1987), 77.

Moses, they were strong, God-centered leaders who confronted the intimidations of the proud world around them. They conquered their imperfections and experienced the deliverance of their Lord. As a result their faith and hope were in God's reversal of worldly expectations: his humiliation of the proud and exaltation of the humble.

Proverbs: Humiliation of Pride versus Exaltation of Humility

Proverbs reemphasizes the lessons of Job and the Psalms. Ungodly arrogance characterizes wicked opponents of God, as evidenced by their haughty eyes and proud heart (Prov. 6:16; 21:4, 23–34, with Pss. 101:5; 119:21, 49–52, 69–70, 85–86 in contrast to Job-like humility in 131:1). Consequently, God and his people hate evil, which is rooted in pride (Prov. 8:13).

However, the book distinctively emphasizes the counterintuitive reversal of fortunes; namely, God exalts humble believers and abases proud oppressors. The principle appears initially in Proverbs 3:33–35 (cf. 15:25):

> The Lord's curse is on the house of the wicked,
>> but he blesses the dwelling of the righteous.
> Toward the scorners he is scornful,
>> but to the humble he gives favor.
> The wise will inherit honor,
>> but fools get disgrace.

The passage parallels the humble and the wise to introduce humility as a primary component of "the way of wisdom," a central concern of the book. The blessings of wise living are tested first in the home. Only if that relational base is healthy can people nurture an honorable reputation in their community.

A scorn-filled dwelling is a disgraceful curse, while a God-honoring family reflects teachable children and wise parents. The emphasis is the proverbial "pride goes before a fall, but humility is the way to honor" (cf. 16:18). In other words, pride "falls" because it is so focused on short-term self-interests that it ignores godly concerns that bestow the honor of loving relationships.

Beyond Proverbs, James 4 and 1 Peter 5 quote this passage and, with the example of Christ, elevate the principle to a defining characteristic of godly living:

> Therefore whoever wishes to be a friend of the world makes himself an enemy of God. Or do you suppose it is to no purpose that the Scripture says, "He yearns jealously over the spirit that he has made to dwell in us"? But he gives more grace. Therefore it says, "God opposes the proud, but gives grace to the humble." Submit yourselves therefore to God. (James 4:4–7; cf. 1 John 2:15–17)

> Clothe yourselves, all of you, with humility toward one another, for "God opposes the proud but gives grace to the humble." Humble yourselves, therefore, under the mighty hand of God so that at the proper time he may exalt you. (1 Peter 5:5–6)

James 4:5 attributes humility to God's indwelling Spirit. We are reminded that humility must be defined as God-centered living. This verse is difficult to translate and interpret; its quotation appears to be a general reference to a scriptural principle— namely, "God yearns for the humble devotion of his people." The Spirit expresses this passion for the believer's heart, and God's grace enables humble living in spite of the powerful influence of worldly pride.[20] Peter connected humility under God

20. Cf. Leslie Mitton, *The Epistle of James* (Grand Rapids: Eerdmans, 1966), 153–58.

with humility among believers, implying that submission to God enables gracious attitudes among his people. We are to be constantly clothed with reciprocal humility as we trust God for the strength of his grace in our suffering.[21] Both passages remind us that humility is a loving virtue that is only possible with God-centered living.

The reversal of fortunes appears elsewhere in Proverbs 11:2: "When pride comes, then comes disgrace, but with the humble is wisdom." Similarly, 13:10 states, "By insolence comes nothing but strife, but with those who take advice is wisdom." This reminds us that teachability is a basic characteristic of humble living. The arrogant person is incorrigible, always engendering strife because he is stubbornly enslaved to his own rightness. "This is the conceited supercilious ass who spoils everything which he touches, who is ham-fisted and wrong-headed and can be depended on to create strife, wound feelings and inflame passions."[22] And in the words of 29:23, "One's pride will bring him low, but he who is lowly in spirit will obtain honor." 15:25–33 uses this principle to distinguish wicked from godly lifestyles. The passage begins, "The LORD tears down the house of the proud." Pride is manifested in egotistical thoughts, greed for unjust gain, slanderous speech, and a refusal to listen to wisdom. On the other hand, righteous people are gracious in speech, practice justice, and heed wisdom.[23] The passage concludes with "the

21. James Price concluded: "In summary, both the disposition of humility which one brings to relationships with others and a basic humility before God are closely joined. . . . The fundamental submission to God (cf. 1 Pt. 5:6) is the source for the moral disposition of humility. We may conclude, then, that actually there is not a fundamental difference between the humility concepts in 1 Peter 5:5b and 5:6." "Submission-Humility in 1 Peter: An Exegetical Study" (PhD diss., Vanderbilt University, 1977), 281–82.

22. "Pride is always something which causes nothing but quarrel and strife, for the root of pride is egoism." William McKane, *Proverbs: A New Approach* (Philadelphia: Westminster, 1970), 454. Also, Franz Delitzsch, *Biblical Commentary on the Proverbs of Solomon*, trans. M. G. Easton, 2 vols. (Grand Rapids: Eerdmans, 1968), 1:276.

23. "The special evil of pride is that it opposes the first principle of wisdom (the

fear of the Lord is instruction in wisdom, and humility comes before honor" (v. 33).

We began with the perennially popular view that Job suffered because he was guilty of pride; "who sinned, this man or his parents, that he was born blind?" (John 9:1). The Lord challenged Job to bring arrogant forces down as he does. Of course, Job had to acknowledge that only divine grace can penetrate such deeply ingrained sin. He submitted to God's wisdom and was exalted in the end. Psalms and Proverbs presented pride and humility in terms of wicked and righteous people, respectively. Believers, in humility, were not to retaliate against their ungodly oppressors. Instead they were to trust God for his just intervention on their behalf. This was a proactive response to prideful adversaries, but it required a staunch confidence in the real presence of God as their refuge. Proverbs reveals that God abases the proud and rewards believers for their trust in him.

Joseph and Daniel illustrate wisdom's teaching on humility. Joseph responded to the aggressions of Potiphar's wife with, "How then can I do this great wickedness and sin against God?" (Gen. 39:9). For the injustice of prison, the Lord granted Joseph favor in the sight of the warden (v. 21). In the end, after years of treachery and stressful leadership, he told his brothers, "So it was not you who sent me here, but God. He has made me a father to Pharaoh, and lord of all his house and ruler over all the land of Egypt" (45:8). This is the promise of biblical humility—an exaltation that is devoid of egoism or self-aggrandizement. Joseph suffered repeatedly in circumstances that would have embittered prideful people, but his confidence in God gave him wise gifts that led to places of honor in God's providence. Daniel, who persevered

---

fear of the Lord) and the two great commandments. The proud man is therefore at odds with himself (8:36), his neighbour (13:10), and the Lord (16:5). *Destruction* may appropriately come from any quarter." Derek Kidner, *The Proverbs: An Introduction and Commentary* (Downers Grove: Inter-Varsity, 1964), 120.

in faith and prayer, testified, "My God sent his angel and shut the lions' mouths," while those who maliciously accused Daniel did not even reach the bottom of the den before "the lions over-powered them and broke all their bones in pieces" (Dan. 6:22, 24). Daniel gave glory to God and was honored by Darius. His adversaries, who maliciously plotted against him and the Lord, were destroyed in the judgment that they had sought for him.

The lessons of Israel's wisdom are not consigned to the crypt of antiquity. They reflect humanity's approach to sin and its consequences in any age. Nancy Gibbs is one of America's most insightful and articulate journalists. In 2009, she lamented our "Age of Arrogance" and called for humility:

> The problems we face are too fierce to accommodate arrogance. Humility leaves room for complexity, honors honest dissent, welcomes the outlandish idea that sweeps past ideology and finds invention.... The odds are much better if we come to the table assuming we don't already have all the answers.[24]

Gibbs correctly pegged the problem of arrogance, but she tragically left God out of her appeal. She asks the public that created the problem to reverse its momentum and admit the vanity of its humanistic strivings. Her call has fallen on deaf ears, because deeply ingrained sin can only be transformed by divine grace. The self-aggrandizement of our age dismisses trust in God as worthless and inconsequential. Our drives for purpose and significance are crushed between the so-called promises of technological innovation and the despair of moral decay. Allender and Longman correctly point us to God, who made us and "stoops down to lift us up to the glory in which we were meant to be clothed."[25] In accord with an important biblical emphasis,

24. Nancy Gibbs, "The Age of Arrogance," *Time* (November 9, 2009), 64.
25. Allender and Longman , *The Cry of the Soul*, 255.

the authors' language reminds us that God exemplifies the life that he commands us to follow; he stoops in humility to deliver his people from the curses of pride. Just as God exposes and judges godless pride, so he promises to exalt godly humility. Joseph and Daniel demonstrated that this is the way of wisdom.

Summary

Job teaches that godly people may suffer intensely. Suffering is not necessarily caused by unconfessed sin, and prosperity is not necessarily an indicator of God's blessing on the righteous. Job was a "righteous sufferer." Ultimately, some circumstances are seemingly beyond our understanding and control. In the Psalms worldly persecutors appeared to have gained riches by oppressing the poor. Proverbs counsels prayer for the oppressed, because vengeance is God's prerogative, and he promises to exalt humble believers. The importance of Wisdom Literature is evidenced by the New Testament's numerous quotations from it, supporting the timeless need for submission to our good God.

Key Terms

land of blessing. God's promise of a land for Israel that would be their home.
perseverance. Holding to a course or direction in life with steadfastness.
poor. "Poor [humble] in spirit" rather than poverty in property from laziness or reckless living.
psalms of lament. The cries of believers to God for deliverance from godless persecutors.
supercilious. Showing arrogant disdain for another person.
theocracy. The governance of Israel by God.
vengeance. Inflicting harm on unjust adversaries.

vindication. To justify or support one's claim.

wisdom. The God-given skill of understanding how life should be lived.

Questions for Discussion

1. What does the Bible mean when it affirms that the ways of the world (pride) end in death?
2. Why are popular notions about suffering being caused by sin "the real charade"?
3. What is the hinge (turning point) of the book of Job?
4. What was Satan's strategy in his interview with God? Did Job curse God to his face (Job 1:11)?
5. How did Jesus' answer in John 9 clarify God's use of suffering? At the end of John 9, how many people worshipped Jesus?
6. How does the crucifixion of Jesus parallel Job on the principle that God will exalt his humble servants?
7. Is biblical faith in the biblical God absolutely necessary for true wisdom about life?
8. Why do the wicked prosper?
9. Do you think that the wicked Israelites in the Psalms felt that they were invulnerable because they did not believe that God existed? Were they so haughty that they attacked their king as well?
10. Why is the transition from lament to praise in the Psalms unique to Israel, and what does this indicate about God's purposes in our struggles?
11. What is "legitimate pride" in the Bible?
12. A central emphasis of biblical wisdom is a "counterintuitive reversal of outcomes." What does this mean in Proverbs?
13. Does a life of pride always "fall," and if so, how and why?
14. How do Joseph and Daniel illustrate wisdom's teaching on God's exaltation of humility?

For Further Reading

Allender, Dan, and Tremper Longman III. *The Cry of the Soul: How Our Emotions Reveal Our Deepest Questions about God.* Colorado Springs: NavPress, 1994. An important exposition of the Psalms with noteworthy parallels to this chapter.

Morgan, Christopher W., and Robert Peterson, eds. *Fallen: A Theology of Sin.* Wheaton, IL: Crossway, 2013. Contributions by Paul House ("Law, Writings, and Prophets"), Ralph Yarbrough ("Gospels"), and Douglas Moo ("Pauline Epistles") parallel our focus on biblical theology.

4

The Oracles against Pride in the Prophets

IN 1816 GIOVANNI BELZONI, Italian adventurer, acquired a colossal statue of Rameses for the British Museum. As the statue was transported to England in 1818, Percy Bysshe Shelley and Horace Smith challenged each other to write competitive sonnets in *The Examiner*. The pedestal of the statue paraphrased the inscription of Diodorus Siculus, which read "King of Kings am I, Ozymandius"—a Greek transliteration of Rameses's throne name. Shelley's sonnet became his most famous short poem:

> I met a traveler from an antique land
> Who said: "two vast and trunkless legs of stone
> Stand in the desert. Near them, on the sand,
> Half sunk, a shattered visage lies, whose frown
> and wrinkled lip, and sneer of cold command" . . .
> "My name is Ozymandius, king of kings:
> Look on my works, ye mighty, and despair!"
> Nothing beside remains. Round the decay

Of that colossal wreck, boundless and bare
The lone and level sands stretch far away.[1]

Smith's poem was remarkably similar, but it is even more apropos for the subject of pride in the prophets:

"I am great OZYMANDIUS," saith the stone,
"The King of Kings: this mighty City shows
The Wonders of my hand." The City's gone,
Nought but the Leg remaining to disclose
The site of this forgotten Babylon.[2]

We too will reflect on Ozymandius through the lenses of Ezekiel, Isaiah, and Daniel.

The prophets carry principles from the Pentateuch and Wisdom Literature forward. They rivet our attention on imperial cities and their rulers, who epitomize the humiliation-of-pride and exaltation-of-humility under the sovereign direction of the living God. Their unique oracles, taunts, and laments move from the principle of reversal to imperial arrogance and the life-and-death consequences of humble or proud attitudes respectively.

We have seen wisdom's "the Lord lifts up the humble; he casts the wicked to the ground" (Ps. 147:6). In the words of Hans-Helmut Esser, "It is God himself by his acts in history who brings down the proud and arrogant, and chooses and rescues the humiliated."[3] Isaiah directs our attention to the day of the LORD, when "the haughty looks of man shall be brought low, and the lofty pride of men shall be humbled, and the LORD alone will

1. Percy Bysshe Shelley, "Ozymandias," from *The Selected Poetry and Prose of Shelley* (Ware, UK: Wordsworth Poetry Library, 2002).
2. Horace Smith, "Ozymandias," from *Amarynthus, The Nympholet: A Pastoral Drama, In Three Acts. With Other Poems* (1821; repr., New York: Garland Publishing, 1997).
3. *NIDNTT*, s.v. "Humility," by Hans-Helmut Esser, 2:260.

be exalted in that day" (Isa. 2:11; cf. 17). The LORD's exaltation is connected to Israel's idolatry, which indicated an absence of God-centered humility in the nation. According to Ezekiel, the "Sovereign LORD" announced that "all the trees of the field shall know that I am the LORD; I will bring low the high tree, and make high the low tree, dry up the green tree, and make the dry tree flourish" (17:24).

The arrogance of tyrannical leaders and their fawning followers was noted in the Psalms, and attention was directed at Pharaoh and Egypt in the Pentateuch. The overweening presumption of Babel's bid for a great name apart from God became the foundation of Babylon's indictment in Isaiah 14 and Daniel 3–4. Also, with Tyre and its king we can see a hubris that negated humility. Ezekiel in particular traced sin to its prideful roots in Eden. He showed that the godlessness of pride—as opposed to the godly submission of humility—lies at the core of original sin, which became innate in a fallen world where the "survival of the fittest" is a way of life. The presumption of acting as gods, as masters of our life and destiny, is the root of sin that has prompted catastrophic judgments throughout history. The ultimate consequence is death, which represented a great divorce from the living Standard, who expected his people to preserve their covenantal relationships by remembering God's goodness through uncompromised worship.

The prophetic oracles can be synthesized using Ezekiel 28 as a central text because it is the most detailed condemnation of pride. Ezekiel's prophecy against Tyre's king will serve as a prelude to Isaiah's condemnation of the king of Babylon. The emphases of both oracles are illustrated in Daniel 3 and 4. We will develop our discussion in this order:

1. Ezekiel's Oracle against Tyre
2. Isaiah's Oracle against Babylon

3. Daniel's Account of Nebuchadnezzar's Humiliation
4. The Kings' Lessons for Us

The prophets lived in times of international upheaval. In 612 B.C. the great Assyrian city of Nineveh fell to a combined force of Babylonians and Medes. Three years later Egypt sought to reestablish hegemony over Canaan, but in 605 B.C. the Babylonians overwhelmed the Egyptians at Carchemish (cf. Jer. 46:2). Nebuchadnezzar ascended the Babylonian throne and subdued Jerusalem in 597 B.C. King Jehoichin and about ten thousand Jews, including Ezekiel, were exiled to Babylon. In response to further rebellion, the Mesopotamian empire plundered and burned Jerusalem. Ezekiel was a priest and prophet who was called to minister to the exiles, which would have placed him at the nexus of the international upheavals.

Ezekiel's Oracle against Tyre

Ezekiel's judgment against Tyre is found in chapters 26 through 28, a carefully structured passage that uses corporate metaphors of city and king to address a specific location and individual as well as the general sinful human condition.[4] The city-state was on the Mediterranean coast, about one hundred miles northwest of Jerusalem. Though comparatively small, Tyre was proverbially wealthy and powerful, with Ezekiel's images reappearing in Revelation 18 in God's judgment on "Mystery Babylon the Great." For example, in verses 16 through 18,

"Alas, alas, for the great city . . . !

4. The collection of oracles is organized into three units by a concluding refrain: chaps. 26, 27, and 28, the latter pairing distinguishable oracles. Tyre means "rock," which suggests its geographical location as well as its security. Prophecies against Tyre also occur in: Isaiah 23, Jeremiah 25, 47, Joel 3, Amos 1, and Zechariah 9.

For in a single hour all this wealth has been laid waste."

And all shipmasters and seafaring men, sailors and all whose trade is on the sea, stood far off and cried out as they saw the smoke of her burning,
"What city was like the great city?"

And they threw dust on their heads as they wept and mourned, crying out,

"Alas, alas, for the great city
where all who had ships at sea
grew rich by her wealth!
For in a single hour she has been laid waste."

Tyre had two ports that were joined by a causeway; the mainland port profited from overland trading and its offshore counterpart, a rocky island about a half mile from the coast, was a gateway for maritime trade. Accordingly, its economic power and defensive capabilities gave it an attitude of invulnerability. However, Babylonian forces under Nebuchadnezzar destroyed the mainland part of the city (Ezek. 26:7), while the island survived until an invasion by Alexander the Great in the fourth century.

Ezekiel 26 pronounced judgment against the city, while chapter 27 described Tyre's fall through an extended metaphor of a sinking ship, which magnified the calamitous shipwreck (vv. 25–36). The cause of judgment was the city-state's presumptuous celebration of Jerusalem's fall in 586 B.C., when it said, "'Aha, the gate of the peoples is broken; it has swung open to me. I shall be replenished, now that she is laid waste,' therefore thus says the Lord GOD: Behold, I am against you, O Tyre" (26:2–3; cf. Jer. 52:12). The "gate of the peoples" refers to Jerusalem's strategic proximity to international trade routes. Instead of grief for a former ally, the Tyrians saw a selfish advantage for a greater share of the revenues. Wealth is power, and greed creates an arrogant spirit of invincibility. The city-state trusted in its own strengths and became oblivious to the sovereignty of the Lord GOD.

So that "they will know that I am the LORD," God used Nebuchadnezzar, king of Babylon, to plunder Tyre's wealth (Ezek. 26:6, 12). In 585 B.C. this would have meant that the funeral dirge predicted the inevitability of the mainland's demise. The judgment is compared to the flood in Genesis (vv. 19–21). Death is the destiny of greed, so, as with the flood, the Lord "will make you go down with those who go down to the pit, to the people of old, and I will make you to dwell in the world below, among ruins from of old, with those who go down to the pit, so that you will not be inhabited; . . . I will bring you to a dreadful end" (vv. 20–21).[5] The curse raised the case against Tyre to a general condemnation of arrogance and its corollary greed. The sovereign Judge decreed the city's fate. The same God, we must note, offers a living hope for a permanent, enduring city for his people (cf. Zeph. 2:3; 3:11–12; Heb. 11:10).

Allies had profited from Tyre's godless gain, and they led the lamentation over their loss (Ezek. 26:16; cf. 27:28–36): "Then all the princes of the sea will step down from their thrones and remove their robes and strip off their embroidered garments. They will clothe themselves with trembling; they will sit on the ground and tremble every moment and be appalled at you." The death of the city and the loss of affluence underscore the magnitude of sin's destruction (cf. 26:17–18). An invincible ship (chap. 27) on the mighty seas exposed the enemies of God as the truly vulnerable in the world.[6]

---

5. Tyre's descent to the world below is repeated more elaborately in the destiny of mighty, uncircumcised nations (Ezek. 32:9–10) in the prophet's lament over Egypt. The connecting theme is God's humiliation of proud rulers with a "dreadful end."

6. Cf. E. M. Good, "Ezekiel's Ship: Some Extended Metaphors in the Old Testament,"

The poetry of Ezekiel 27 is interrupted by prose narrative (vv. 10–25), which heightens the disastrous shipwreck. Tyre had boasted about its extraordinary beauty: "O Tyre, you have said, 'I am perfect in beauty.' . . . Your builders made perfect your beauty" (vv. 3–4). Skilled shipbuilders used only the finest materials to build "the ship," and only the best of merchant seamen navigated its routes. Fame and strength, however, bring formidable temptations, and "the temptation to pride is enormous, precisely because of the great work and skill. . . . But, like rot in the hull of a great ship, pride will lead eventually to shipwreck."[7] Heavily ladened in the heart of the high seas, the ship was battered in a storm and sank. The flotsam washed ashore, provoking lamentation over the loss of wealth that had enriched kings. Storms are beyond human control and expose the weakness of arrogant traders, but they inspire trust in almighty God who alone can still the seas (cf. Ps. 89:9; Prov. 3:7; 26:12).

The pride of the city is exemplified by its ruler in Ezekiel 28:1–10. The oracle condemns the ruler for his presumption in making divine claims: "Because your heart is proud, and you have said, 'I am a god, I sit in the seat of the gods, in the heart of the seas'" (v. 2).[8] In the ancient Near East, wisdom was understood practically as the skill of mastering life. So, because he had demonstrated wisdom in acquiring wealth, his heart was inflated into a prosperous future without limits. In Mesopotamia and Phoenicia, kings were viewed generally as instruments of divine

---

Semitics 1 (1970): 79–103. The city's sudden destruction at the height of its power suggests the fragility of power apart from God (cf. Zech. 4:6). The "east wind" in Ezekiel 27:26 should be understood as God's breath of judgment, as in Isaiah 27:8.

7. Peter Craigie, *Ezekiel*, Daily Study Bible Series (Philadelphia: Westminster, 1983), 199.

8. "You have made your heart like the heart of God" is an antithetical counterpoint to Christ's humility in Philippians 2:6–7: "Who, being in very nature God . . . made himself nothing" (NIV).

authority. The extraordinary achievements of this ruler led him from reality to a delusion of deity. Walther Zimmerli notes the transition: "It affirms with secret horror how, out of this good gift, which to begin with led to rich success and the wonderful expansion of the potentiality of human life, there has grown the bitter fruit of pride that makes men forget the only lord and giver of all created things."[9] Wealth may indicate worldly wisdom, but wiser than Daniel (v. 3)? The reference seems to allude to the biblical prophet who had a reputation for wisdom that was nuanced by a realization of his dependence on God and his own mortality (cf. 14:14; Dan. 2:46–48).[10] With sarcasm, Ezekiel underscored the foolishness of pride and materialistic priorities.

An oracle of judgment follows. "Therefore thus says the Lord GOD: Because you make your heart like the heart of a god, therefore, I will bring foreigners upon you . . . and they shall draw their swords against the beauty of your wisdom" (Ezek. 28:6–7). The judgment for hubris is death, which is forcefully presented in terms of the pit and a word play on *yam* ("sea"). Verses 8–10 match the cause with the consequence:

> "They shall thrust you down into the pit,
>> and you shall die the death of the slain
>> in the heart of the seas.
> Will you still say, 'I am a god,'
>> in the presence of those who kill you,

9. Walther Zimmerli, *Ezekiel 2: A Commentary on the Book of the Prophet Ezekiel, Chapters 25–48*, trans. James Martin, Hermeneia (Philadelphia: Fortress, 1983), 80.

10. The verse refers to higher wisdom, secrets, and mysteries that can be known only by divine enablement. "A sarcastic comparison. In xiv. 14 Daniel was mentioned as an outstanding example of piety, here of wisdom. Of him the Babylonian king said, *'No secret causeth thee trouble'* (Dan. iv. 6)." S. Fisch, *Ezekiel: Hebrew Text & English Translation with an Introduction and Commentary*, Soncino Books of the Bible (Jerusalem: Soncino, 1950), 189.

> though you are but a man, and no god,
>   in the hands of those who slay you?
> You shall die the death of the uncircumcised
>   by the hand of foreigners;
>   for I have spoken, declares the Lord GOD."

In Hebrew *yam* is sea, and in Tyrian (Ugaritic) mythology *Yam* is a chaotic god who killed Baal. Ezekiel is poetically emphasizing that the one who would pretend to be divine would die in the midst of the sea. The "heart of the seas," an initial source of wealth, became the grave of Tyre's self-sufficient beauty. Human wisdom can achieve a measure of success, but biblical wisdom is grounded in "the fear of the LORD" and would prohibit divine claims (Prov. 1:7).

Whether he realizes it or not, the ruler is accountable for the ethics of his city-state, so that he must be brought low for his pride (Ps. 101:5; Prov. 16:5; Eccl. 7:8). In the words of Isaiah 25:11, "The LORD will lay low his pompous pride together with the skill of his hands." The prophetic indictment transcends a particular ruler of the city, such as Ithobaal II, with its focus on the attitude of Tyre's "heart," the term used eight times in Ezekiel 28:2–8. From the core of its value system, the city and ruler claimed divine status in hostility to God. The quotation in verse 2 amplifies the charge, "I am a god, I sit in the seat of the gods."[11] The latter claim moves from the ruler's human nature to his delusion that he has sovereign prerogatives over the affairs of the earth. It stands in antithesis to the Lord GOD's oft-repeated claim that he acts in history so that "they will know that I am the LORD."

The Bible draws an unequivocal line between creature and Creator, so the Lord, in spite of the claim (Ezek. 28:2, 9), corrects it with "yet you are but a man, and no god" (v. 2; cf. Isa. 31:3). He

11. Similar is the condemnation of Pharaoh in Ezekiel 29 for the claim, "My Nile is my own; I made it for myself" (v. 3; cf. v. 9).

will bring ruthless enemies to inflict death on the blasphemous ruler (v. 7; cf. 31:12). The dreadful death of the uncircumcised in the pit culminated the ruler's fall from the heights of wisdom and wealth to the ignominious depths of defeat and death (cf. 32:7–12).

A second judgment against the ruler (מֶלֶךְ) follows, and completes the symmetry of double judgments against the city and its king (Ezek. 26–28).[12] The imagery and terminology are distinctive and raise a number of questions about the subjects and scope of the lament. Intuitively, we would have expected the oracles about the ruler of Tyre to be consistent in form and content with the judgments of the city-ship. However, the uniqueness of verses 11–19 leads us to conclude that the ruler points to cosmic dimensions of the problem of pride and its consequences: "But as he [Ezekiel] viewed the thoughts and ways of that monarch, he clearly discerned behind him the motivating force and personality who was impelling him in his opposition to God."[13]

First, the word for "ruler" changes from נָגִיד ("prince," Ezek. 28:1) to מֶלֶךְ ("king," v. 11). *King* is usually a mere designation of the ruling position. The term is used elsewhere in Ezekiel with reference to rulers of countries (17:12; 19:9; 27:33, 35; 29:2). נָגִיד, however, is normally used in connection with God's appointment or delegation of responsibility and connotes an accountability to God for serving in an office—whether king, supervisor, commander, or otherwise. Accordingly, the prince must answer to God for his presumptuousness.[14]

12. Ezekiel 28:11–19 is generally considered to be corrupt textually and very difficult to interpret. Scholarly emendations are based on assumptions about parallels between the form, structure, terminology, and argument of the Tyrian laments. The present passage is unique and can hardly be reconstructed without altering its content. Commentators agree, however, that the humiliation of the proud is its primary theme.

13. Charles Lee Feinberg, *The Prophecy of Ezekiel: The Glory of the Lord* (Chicago: Moody, 1969), 161.

14. A similar emphasis, where מֶלֶךְ is used of Nebuchadnezzar, can be found in Jeremiah 27:2–6 and Daniel 2:37.

Second, an important clue to the larger significance of the passage is the identification of a cherub with distinctive traits that cannot be applied to the human king of Tyre (cf. Ezek. 28:2, 9). The cherubim are guardian angels in the presence of God and occupy a prominent place in Ezekiel. After Adam and Eve were expelled from Eden, God "placed the cherubim and a flaming sword . . . to guard the way to the tree of life" (Gen. 3:24).[15] Golden figures of cherubim adorned the mercy seat of the ark, where the fire and cloud of God's presence led Israel in the tabernacle and temples (e.g., Ex. 25:17–22; 37:7–9; 40:38). The veil that separated the Holy of Holies from the rest of the sanctuary featured embroidered cherubim (1 Kings 6:27; 2 Chron. 3:14; cf. Ezek. 41:15–20, where Ezekiel's visionary temple expands the motif). Particularly important are the heavenly visions in chapters 1 and 10. Cherubim guarded and escorted God's throne-chariot and appeared "like burning coals of fire, like the appearance of torches moving to and fro" (Ezek. 1:13). As the glory of the LORD moved away from the temple, the cherubim "stood at the entrance of the east gate of the house of the LORD, and the glory of the God of Israel was over them" (10:19). With this introduction in view, the LORD proclaimed in 28:14, "You were an anointed guardian cherub."

The precedent of the passage is "Eden, the garden of God" (Ezek. 28:13). Like *cherub*, this explicit reference to the biblical paradise cannot be compared with the proud city and its king, who were hardly "blameless in your ways from the day you were created" (v. 15).[16] The cherub in Eden was further described as

15. Some scholars relate the juxtaposed decorations of cherubim and palm trees in Solomon's temple to the expulsion from Eden.

16. The clarity of the passage has led a number of scholars to a "primeval man" interpretation, in which the guardian cherub is the agent of judgment. This view cannot explain the details of the lament. The literature on the Adamic figure has been surveyed by A. J. Williams, "The Mythical Background of Ezekiel 28:12–19?," *Biblical Theology Bulletin* 6 (1976): 49–61.

"the signet of perfection, full of wisdom and perfect in beauty" (v. 12), which aligns him with the city (27:3) and the ruler (28:7). *Signet* signifies the standard or model of wisdom and beauty. He was adorned with a covering of precious gems that was prepared "from the day you were created" (v. 15).[17] The "fiery stones" (v 14, NIV) seem to refer to the dazzling visions of God's presence in chapter 1.

After describing the cherub, the LORD declared, "I placed you; you were on the holy mountain of God; in the midst of the stones of fire you walked" (28:14). The emphatic statement of God's appointment must be noted to highlight the betrayal of the guardian. "The holy mountain of God" refers to the place of his presence. Psalm 48:1 refers to Zion as "his holy mountain, beautiful in elevation" and "the joy of the earth" (cf. Ezek. 20:40).[18] Interestingly, the psalm also refers to an assembly of kings who fled in terror from the dwelling of God (Ps. 48:4–7) and "by the east wind you shattered the ships of Tarshish" (v. 7). And Isaiah refers to worship on the "holy mountain at Jerusalem" (Isa. 27:13), the mountain of his dwelling from which he will bless the earth (25:4–10).

How do we reconcile the king of Tyre with the garden of Eden in a way that plausibly relates Ezekiel and Genesis? The answer lies in a biblical understanding of temptation, the common denominator of pride, and the respective judgments of the guilty parties.[19] We should recall the fall and expulsion from Eden

17. Interpreters have speculated at length on the covering, but these matters do not concern us beyond their relation to his beauty.

18. Note Ezekiel's point about Jerusalem as the "center of the nations" and "the center of the earth" (5:5 and 38:12, respectively), the "navel" from which God's sovereignty extended to the ends of the earth. This emphasis brings into focus the cause of judgment in 26:2–3, which was discussed earlier.

19. Jon Leverson, at the time professor of the Hebrew Bible at the University of Chicago's Divinity School, reviewed Greenberg's *Ezekiel 1–20* and Zimmerli's *Ezekiel 2* in *Interpretation* 38 (1984): 210–17. He offered the following observation, which accounts for problematic interpretations of Ezekiel's oracle against Tyre and its king:

from our earlier discussion of the Pentateuch. A fellow creature tempted Adam and Eve through a serpent.[20] The temptation was directed at their exalted creation in the image of God, which bestowed an innate ambition to rule (Gen. 1:26). In other words, Adam was a prototypical ruler over creation under God, and as a fallen ruler he was the father of other princes for whom the presumption of deity was even more irresistible, including the rulers of Tyre and Babylon.[21] Walther Eichrodt makes this point: "The reproach addressed to him does not reveal any personal details about his character or his political policy, but is couched in terms so general that any Tyrian king might have served as its target. It is rather that the kingship *per se* is being prosecuted and

---

"The factor which most sharply distinguishes the modern, critical study of the Bible from its pre-modern antecedents, Jewish or Christian, is the acute awareness that the text has a history. In the past, the harmonization of ostensible contradictions was, for whatever reason, more credible than it has been since the Enlightenment, at least in elite academic circles. . . . Today, anyone who invokes supernatural causation in such matters is labeled a 'fundamentalist,' even by scholars who persist in calling their scriptures 'the word of God.' Having given up the presumption of textual unity, the historicocritical method seeks the historical information which the harmonization and inconsistencies can only suppress." Levenson's caveat surfaces a neglected distinction between information that is needed to interpret a text properly and our response to premodern beliefs that we might find unacceptable (in this case, demonic beings). In other words, elite academicians (1) will not introduce crucial aspects of the initial chapters of Genesis or Revelation into an understanding of Ezekiel 28, (2) cannot draw from other texts in Ezekiel about cherubim, and (3) will not examine temptation as a contributing factor in the king's fall.

20. "The use of the verb *bara* ('to create') brings the creature described here into the context of a statement about creation. This creature, with which the king of Tyre is compared, has about it the dignity and splendor of the primeval." Zimmerli, *Ezekiel 2*, 92. Carol Newsom insightfully notes, "The imagery of the present oracle, however, goes beyond a claim of Yahweh's ability to break Tyre's power to assert in some way Yahweh is the creator of all true advantages which Tyre possesses." "A Maker of Metaphors—Ezekiel's Oracles Against Tyre," *Interpretation* 38 (1984): 161.

21. For example, when Herod was angry with the people of Tyre and Sidon in Acts 12, they gained an audience with him because they depended on him for food: "On an appointed day Herod put on his royal robes, took his seat upon the throne, and delivered an oration to them. And the people were shouting, 'The voice of a god, and not of a man!' Immediately an angel of the Lord struck him down, because he did not give God the glory, and he was eaten by worms and breathed his last" (vv. 21–23).

sentenced in the person of its representative."[22] Adam and Eve were deceitfully promised that they could acquire a divine wisdom that could rule without creaturely limitation.[23] After all, was not the forbidden tree "a delight to the eyes"?[24] The fallen couple in shame was expelled from the garden, and they bequeathed to future humanity the delusions of divine ambition and the reality of death. This destiny of death for hubris is consistent not only with Ezekiel's teaching (Ezek. 31:14) but also with the rest of the Old Testament (cf. Ps. 82:6) and the Bible as a whole (cf. 2 Thess. 2:3–4 with Rev. 20).

What befell the tempted also cursed the tempter. John identified the adversary of God and humanity as "the great dragon [who] was thrown down, that ancient serpent, who is called the devil and Satan, the deceiver of the whole world" (Rev. 12:9; cf. 20:2). As he used the serpent in Eden, so Satan has been the dragon who promotes chaos in God's creation through presumptuous leadership. Isaiah described God's judgment of the "chaos monster" in 27:1: "In that day the LORD with his hard and great and strong sword will punish Leviathan the fleeing serpent, Leviathan the twisting serpent, and he will slay the dragon that is in the sea." Furthermore, Paul notes that recent converts should

22. Walther Eichrodt, *Ezekiel: A Commentary*, OTL, trans. Cosslett Quin (Philadelphia: Westminster, 1970), 390.

23. The wisdom to succeed found in Ezekiel can be paralleled with the deceitful cunning found in Genesis. Sinners, even saved sinners, characteristically crave more than God has given them, regardless of how successful they may be. Pride makes us insatiable!

24. "What is narrated here as the fate of princes is narrated in terms of primeval man, of man at the beginning, of man pure and simple. He was the one who was richly endowed, summoned to be beside God, adorned with perfect beauty. But he was then the proud one, the one who turned in on himself, who seized for himself and acted highhandedly with what was, as a gift, a great favor." Zimmerli, *Ezekiel 2*, 95. Also, "the prophet's anatomy of evil, and his tracing of the road out of Eden, are as true today as in his own time. Desire, greed, violence, and pride are the scourges of the human race that have removed all signs of Eden from our world. . . . We are made in such a way that we perpetually desire the divine presence in the garden, but we act in such a way that we cannot achieve it." Craigie, *Ezekiel*, 208.

not be overseers, least they "become puffed up with conceit and fall into the condemnation of the devil" (1 Tim. 3:6). Therefore, the distinctive judgments in Ezekiel can be paralleled with the curses in Genesis as well. Evidently both the tempter and tempted were expelled from the garden, and their sins were joined by temptation after the fall. Mankind's prideful rebellion introduced death as the proof of sin through history (cf. Ezek. 3:18–21). People traded beauty for hard labor. The serpent was humiliated to the lowest of all beasts in the dust of the fields. And shadowy Satan was to be mortally defeated by the Son of Man.[25]

Because the tempted and the tempter coalesce in their sin, Satan shares in Ezekiel's condemnation of the ruler of Tyre. In Paul's words, "Put on the whole armor of God, that you may be able to stand against the schemes of the devil. For we do not wrestle against flesh and blood, but against the rulers, against the authorities, against the cosmic powers over this present darkness, against the spiritual forces of evil in the heavenly places" (Eph. 6:11–12). Appropriately, the New Testament refers to Satan as "the ruler of this world" of darkness (John 12:31; 14:30; 16:11; 1 John 5:19; the NIV translates *archon* as "prince") or "the god [*theos*] of this world" (2 Cor. 4:4), meaning that he is a primary motivator to rebellion against God. The designations, of course, are an indictment of his misuse of power, since he was

---

25. We are aware that questions arise that cannot be fully answered with the information at our disposal. Was Satan a guardian angel in Eden, which would have underscored his betrayal of God's trust? Did he, as a cherub, envy Adam's rule over creation, since angels are "ministering spirits sent out to serve for the sake of those who are to inherit salvation" (Heb. 1:14)? Did creatures like the serpent lose an ability to speak, a judgment touching language as at Babel, and did they lose upright posture to grovel on the ground? Ralph Alexander states, "Only by seeing Satan as the force behind Tyre's king and the spirit working in him can we even begin to relate these verses to Satan." *Isaiah–Ezekiel*, ed. Frank E. Gaebelein et al., EBC 6 (Grand Rapids: Zondervan, 1986), 884. That is the point! I do not deny that the king of Tyre is in the foreground and that through him we see the human problem of hubris and consequent divine judgment. I am saying that the balance of Ezekiel and the Bible favor a more complete explanation of the fall from Eden and its abiding consequences.

appointed as a guardian of God's glory. We may reasonably infer that both the king and Satan are condemned for violent trade, as indicated by their presumption against God (Ezek. 28:16). Satan has not been "slain in the heart of the seas," but "as a profane thing was cast from the mountain of God" and expelled as a guardian from "the stones of fire." In Ezekiel this seems to refer to his removal from his cherubic position in the presence of God (chaps. 1 and 10), so that now, as the father of lies, he "disguises himself as an angel of light. So it is no surprise if his servants, also, disguise themselves as servants of righteousness" (2 Cor. 11:14–15). Such is deceit! City, king, and tempter are humiliated and exposed for the multitude of their iniquities that profaned their sanctuaries. In other words, pride lies at the core of a multitude of sins. Their judgment was so dreadful that kings and people were appalled at the horrible remains of what had once been so desirable.

Thus far, we have seen how the prophets continued the emphasis on the Lord's exaltation of the humble and humiliation of the proud. Their images, however, are distinctive and vivid. Ezekiel was a priest and prophet among the exiles in the Babylonian exile. His oracles against Tyre (chaps. 26–28) focus the humiliation of pride on the destruction of a seemingly invulnerable city in the seas that had transported its wealth. The fall of its king was traced to his arrogance in making divine claims about being worldly wise. The allusion to the fall of humanity in Genesis reveals the shadow of a fallen cherub, who had used pride to bring chaos to God's creation. Ezekiel taught that powerful rulers are particularly prone to hubris, but we can infer that personal powers lead all sinners to an excessively exalted view of themselves. The world seeks false immortalities through a great name in this life, but it habitually dismisses its mortality under God. The issue, once again, is humility as God-centeredness, for he acts in history so that "they will know that I am the Lord."

Almost every detail of the oracles is contested, but the undeniable lesson is that pride goes before a fall.

Isaiah's Oracle against Babylon

Scholars frequently compare Isaiah 14:3–21 with Ezekiel 28. The passage is a part of the prophet's oracles against nations in chapters 13–23. These chapters point to worldwide judgment as a prelude to the Lord's kingdom on earth (chaps. 24–27). Besides Isaiah 14, the prophet also addressed Babylon in chapter 21 and Tyre in chapter 23. With these prophecies to Judah, Isaiah exhorted God's people not to seek alliances with powerful nations for security, because God is the Sovereign of the earth and worthy of their trust.

Isaiah 13 introduces the Babylonian oracle with a warning about God's judgment of haughty rulers who oppress their victims:

> The LORD of hosts is mustering a host for battle. . . . Wail, for the day of the LORD is near; as destruction from the Almighty it will come! . . . "I will put an end to the pomp of the arrogant, and lay low the pompous pride of the ruthless. . . . And Babylon, the glory of kingdoms, the splendor and pomp of the Chaldeans will be like Sodom and Gomorrah when God overthrew them. (13:4, 6, 11, 19)[26]

These verses parade a cluster of terms around pride that underscore the Lord's indictment: *arrogance, haughtiness, pomposity,*

---

26. Geoffrey Grogan aptly states: "It is thoroughly characteristic of Isaiah to mention arrogance and pride as prime targets of God's judgment on the wicked (v. 11; cf. 2:11–18; 3:16–24; 10:8–16). Human pride offers a blatant insult to the God who is highly exalted and to whom all his moral creatures should submit in obedient worship." "Isaiah," in *Isaiah–Ezekiel*, ed. Frank E. Gaebelein et al., EBC 6 Grand Rapids: Zondervan, 1986), 102.

and *insolence*. We again encounter the term for arrogance (גאון),
an overweening attitude about one's own importance that leads
to insolent (or ruthless) disrespect of others. Arrogant behavior is also characterized by a haughty appearance that reflects
an inflated sense of self-importance. In a word, proud rulers
are condemned for their disregard of God as the sovereign of
his creation, and this disregard in turn promotes an oppressive
ruthlessness. Isaiah clearly viewed Babylon as the archetypal
perpetrator of imperial pride that promoted rebellion against
God (cf. Gen. 11:1–9; Dan. 4:30; Rev. 17–18), though his condemnation included other kings with similar behavior.

The characteristic name for God in oracles like these is
Shaddai, the Almighty commander of all powers, who will pour
out his wrath on the wickedness of the world in his day. Here "the
day" (Isa. 13:6, 9, 13) is a time of judgment, which apparently began
with the Median conquest of Babylon. The process of desolation
was analogous to Sodom and Gomorrah, whose destruction rendered their lands as uninhabitable except for wild animals (Isa.
13:20–22). Like Ezekiel, Isaiah's judgment of the city is followed by
a curse on its king. In the ancient Near East the ruler corporately
represented the values of the society. The promise of judgment
against the king included deliverance from oppression for God's
exiled people (14:1–2). While the King of Tyre represented the
arrogance of wealth, the king of Babylon was condemned for his
insolent oppression: "How the oppressor has ceased! . . . [who]
ruled the nations in anger with unrelenting persecution" (vv. 4,
6). The exclamation introduces the shock that accompanies the
woeful end of seemingly invincible powers in both passages. Both
kings made claims to deity, but the king of Babylon's pride suggested imperial power more than commercial wisdom.

The taunt begins with nature and nations celebrating his fall
(Isa. 14:7–8). No longer will the cedars of Lebanon be stripped
for the grandeur of his building projects. And "the whole earth

is at rest and quiet; they break forth in singing" (v. 7), a sharp contrast to the silencing of his harps in Sheol (v. 11).

The following scene depicts the king's reception in the realm of the dead rulers (Isa. 14:9–15). Even Sheol was stirred by the arrival of its unexpected inhabitant, and "all who were leaders of the earth" rise to greet him (v. 9), many of whom may have been his victims. They sarcastically reminded him that he had become like them—weak shades in contrast to their former pomp and grandeur. Maggots replaced his royal robes and couches (v. 11). The passage teaches that the consequence of arrogance is death as the great equalizer.

As in Ezekiel, death proved that arrogant people are merely mortal. Royal arrogance in the passage is defined as an attitude of invincibility and the feeling that personal power has achieved deity:

> How you are fallen from heaven,
>   O Day Star, son of Dawn! . . .
> You said in your heart,
>   "I will ascend to heaven;
>   above the stars of God
> I will set my throne on high;
> I will sit on the mount of assembly
>   in the far reaches of the north;
> I will ascend above the heights of the clouds;
> I will make myself like the Most High." (vv. 12–14)

Like the king of Tyre, the king of Babylon's claims are very difficult for modern interpreters, are comprehensive in their allusions to biblical and extrabiblical texts, and contain profound lessons about the danger of pride. Their details, properly understood, expose the heart of pride as the destructive core of fallen humanity.

To begin with, many interpreters have viewed Isaiah 14:12–15 as the fall of Satan. This view cannot be the meaning of the passage because the taunt is directed at the king of Babylon, who is called a man (v. 16) with a physical body (vv. 9–11, 15, 18–20). He is judged with a disgraceful death, in comparison with other kings in Sheol. The imagery of the divine claim is royal: the LORD shattered the king's symbols of power (the staff and scepter, v. 5), and "I will set my throne on high" was at the heart of the king's claim (v. 13). The delusion of divine status is structured around a polarization of the height of God-defying arrogance and the depth of destiny. The initial line resumes the exclamatory shock of the king's fall (vv. 4, 12). The pompous conqueror, who had "laid the nations low" (v. 12), was now humiliated by God, without "name and remnant, descendants and posterity" (v. 22). The following synonymous stanzas emphasize the sinful attitude behind his "being cut down to the ground" (v. 12) in death. In language like the Babel builders in Genesis 11, he vowed to ascend above the heavenly stars and clouds and sit among the divine assembly to sovereignly control the affairs of the earth.[27] Like the king of Tyre, the Babylonian king failed to

27. The king's claim reflected the view of his polytheistic culture. Scholars note that the imagery reflects Ugaritic (West Semitic) and Babylonian mythologies. The gods assembled on their mountain dwelling in the north to determine affairs of the cosmos. The king, a creature, aspired to deity "like the Most High." For example, in the Babylonian creation epic Marduk demanded supremacy in the divine assembly for avenging Tiamat: "Set up the assembly, proclaim supreme my destiny!" James Pritchard, ed., *Ancient Near Eastern Texts Relating to the Old Testament*, 2nd ed., trans. E. A. Speiser (Princeton: Princeton University Press, 1950), 64. Marduk, the patron god of Babylon, perhaps mirrors the claims of the city's ruler as in the tandem of the LORD and David's lineage. This suggests that Isaiah's taunt may have been directed against Babylon's "sovereign" god without denying that the passage also addressed the human king (cf. Isa. 21:9; Zeph. 2:10–11).

The king's pride comes to the fore in his self-centered resolve, "I will make myself." Of course, Isaiah's use of the imagery was polemical, looking back to the garden, the expulsion for prideful disobedience, and the scattering of "the great city." Scholars also note that the "Day Star, son of Dawn" may be an allusion to the Ugaritic Shachar and Helel, the latter of whom rebelled against El and was cast into the underworld.

acknowledge the gift of kingship from Israel's sovereign Creator. He trusted in his own resolve and accomplishments for the attainment of freedom from limitations. Instead, as with Tyre's king, he compromised the emphatic biblical distinction between creature and Creator.

The destiny of the king follows the taunt (Isa. 14:16–22). "But," Isaiah declares, "you are brought down to Sheol, to the far reaches of the pit" (v. 15). His audience was amazed at his exposed corpse, the opposite extreme from his pompous, royal audiences. "Is this the man who made the earth tremble, who shook kingdoms, who made the world like a desert and overthrew its cities, who did not let his prisoners go home?" (vv. 16–17). In contrast to other kings, his corpse was cast away "like a dead body trampled underfoot," because he even "destroyed [his] land ... and people" (vv. 19–20). So the LORD of hosts will sweep Babylon with "the broom of destruction," lest the king's posterity "fill the face of the world with [their kind of] cities" (v. 21). One could hardly imagine a more severe curse for pride, or any other sin for that matter!

Can we identify the Babylonian king? The question is linked to the dating of the oracle. The oracles connect Assyrian and Chaldean kingship under Mesopotamian (or Babylonian) dominion, as the Pentateuch does in Genesis 10:8–10 (cf. Isa. 14:24–27; Jer. 50:17–18). Assyria ruled Babylon in Isaiah's time, and the Medes are explicitly mentioned as agents of judgment in Isaiah 13:17 and 21:2. The king is portrayed as a fearsome conqueror (14:4–7), but he is never identified by Isaiah, who also pictured the

Robert Chisholm observes, "If Zaphon here symbolizes Mount Zion (see Ps. 48:2), it is possible that the reality underlying the mythological imagery is Nebuchadnezzar's assault upon Jerusalem and his desecration of the temple." *Handbook on the Prophets* (Grand Rapids: Baker Academic, 2002), 51. Biblical imagery even used the Day Star image of Messiah as the true hope of the world (cf. Num. 24:17; 2 Sam 23:3–4; 2 Peter 1:19; Rev. 2:28; 22:16). This indicates that the king of Babylon was a false hope who should not have been trusted by believers in Isaiah's day.

city as completely destroyed analogous to Sodom and Gomorrah. Some scholars argue that the prophet was referring to Sennacherib's desecration of the city in 689 B.C., which is mentioned in 23:13.[28] An alternative view is that Isaiah prophesied the fall of Babylon to the Persians under Cyrus in 529 B.C.[29] However, no single event accounts for the fall of a Babylonian conqueror, the desolation of the city, and Israel's freedom from oppression. Just as the taunt expressed the hubris of the city and its gods, so Nebuchadnezzar (605–562 B.C.) represented the image and spirit of the king. He appeared in Ezekiel 26:7–11 as a conqueror, led Babylon to imperial power, and was the clearest biblical illustration of God's humiliation of pride (Dan. 4:37). We do not need to specifically identify the arrogant tyrant in Isaiah 14 beyond that he was a Nebuchadnezzar-like representation of Babylonian arrogance who claimed divine prerogatives in historical and archetypical perspectives.[30]

Babylon's fall was expanded to worldwide judgment in both Isaiah and Revelation. The issue of "Fallen, fallen is Babylon the great! . . . Alas, alas for the great city" (Rev. 18:2, 16) again raises the question of whether Satan should be viewed in relation to the oracle. He was not mentioned by Isaiah, and the context offers no clue such as the cherub did in Ezekiel 28. On the other hand, the Babylonian conqueror reflected the activity of the dragon, who promoted chaos in God's creation (Rev. 12:9; cf. 20:2 with Isa. 27:1). Hence, the divine claims of "a throne on high" reflected the same power who tempted the king of Tyre to claim divine

28. Seth Erlandsson, *The Burden of Babylon: A Study of Isaiah 13:2–14:23* (Lund: Gleerup, 1970), 89–93, 161–66.

29. Chisholm, *Handbook of the Prophets*, 52–53.

30. "We are not to understand any of the individual Babylonian kings as specifically ever having uttered precisely these words, but what they express is rather the intention of the Babylonian power or spirit." E. J. Young, *The Book of Isaiah*, 2 vols., 2nd ed., NICOT, 1:442. The Babylonian Talmud identified the king of Babylon with Nebuchadnezzar. Isadore Epstein, ed., *The Babylonian Talmud*, 18 vols. (London: Soncino, 1938), Tractate Shabbath 49b, Tractate Pesahim 94b, Tractate Hullin 89a.

status with pride in wealth.[31] In the words of H. C. Leupold, "Equally much to the point is *Delitzsch*'s remark that a measure of 'self-deification after the manner of the devil and as a forerunner of the Antichrist' are to be found here (cf. Dan. 11:36 and 2 Thess. 2:4)."[32] Tyre and Babylon, through the lenses of the past and the apocalyptic future, demonstrate how the LORD of hosts has purposed to humble those who walk in pride.

We have seen a second city and king, like Tyre, whose pride was exemplified by ruthless conquest and was judged by Almighty God. Biblical condemnations of Babylon's arrogance stretch from Genesis through Isaiah to the apocalyptic judgments of "the great city" under the Antichrist in Revelation. The king of Babylon, seemingly invincible, shocked the world and underworld with his ignominious death. He who would set his throne on high was reduced to death without dignity. Like his Tyrian counterpart, he was judged "so that they will know that I am the LORD." And, like his counterpart, his arrogance pointed to a shadowy tempter who has vainly sought to subvert God's sovereignty in his creation.

Daniel's Account of Nebuchadnezzar's Humiliation

Nebuchadnezzar's pride and fall appear in Daniel 3 and 4, related chapters demonstrating that "the Most High rules the

31. "Nothing could be more appropriate, for the pride of the king of Babylon was truly satanic. When Satan works his malign will through rulers of this world, he reproduces his own wicked qualities in them, so that they become virtual shadows of which he is the substance. To interpret v. 12 and the following verses in this way means that the passage points to Satan, not directly, but indirectly, much like the way the kings of the line of David point to Christ. All rulers of international significance whose overweening pride and arrogance bring them to ruin under the hand of God's judgment illustrate both the satanic and the Antichrist principles, for these principles are really one." Grogan, "Isaiah," 105.

32. H. C. Leupold, *Exposition of Isaiah*, 2 vols. (Grand Rapids: Baker Books, 1968), 1:260.

kingdom of men and gives to whom he will and sets over it the lowliest of men" (4:17).[33] The third chapter describes the king's monumental, gold-plated statue (ninety by nine feet), which he set up on the plain of Dura in the province of Babylon. We do not know the precise representation of the image, but clearly it was an object of idolatrous worship designed to unify the king's empire (3:6–7, 12). The statue may have represented the king or his gods such as Nabu, the patron deity behind his name. The location on the Babylonian plain recalls the tower of Babel, which was also designed as a unifying center of the inhabited earth (Gen. 11:2, 4). Shadrach, Meshach, and Abednego, godly administrators under Nebuchadnezzar, ignored the king's order and were charged with disobeying the king and not serving his gods (Dan. 3:12). They responded that "the God we serve is able to deliver us from it, and he will deliver us from Your Majesty's hand. But even if he does not, we want you to know, Your Majesty, that we will not serve your gods or worship the image of gold you have set up" (v. 17–18, NIV). God saved them without singed hair or odors from the fire. Consequently, Nebuchadnezzar pronounced a death sentence for anyone who spoke against their God, "for there is no other god who is able to rescue in this way" (v. 29). God delivered his humble servants when the idols were deafeningly silent.

Daniel 4 assumes knowledge of this episode with Nebuchadnezzar's autobiographic account of "the signs and wonders that the Most High God has done for me" (v. 2). It is an imperial proclamation to the same group who had been summoned to worship the image (4:1; 3:7), a praise narrative recording Nebuchadnezzar's dream, arrogance, and humiliation by God. He changed from a persecutor of the King's faithful to a proclaimer

---

33. John Goldingay writes, "Nebuchadnezzar is an example—a warning of how not to be led astray by power and achievement, a model of how to respond to chastisement and humiliation." *Daniel*, vol. WBC 30 (Dallas: Word, 1989), 97.

of God's everlasting dominion over the earth. He recalled that he was "at ease in my house and prospering in my palace" (v. 4) when he received a fearful dream. He turned to Daniel (known as Belteshazzar in the Babylonian court) because he knew that "the spirit of the holy gods" was in him (v. 8). In the king's dream "a tree [was] in the midst of the earth, and its height was great. The tree grew and became strong, and its top reached to heaven, and it was visible to the ends of the whole earth" (vv. 10–11). It provided food and shelter for all flesh. A watchman, an angel of judgment, came down from heaven and commanded that the tree be cut to a stump with a band of iron and bronze around it (vv. 13–15). Verses 16 and 17 indicate that the tree and stump symbolized a person, a common symbol for an emperor: "Let his mind be changed from a man's, and let a beast's mind be given to him; and let seven periods of time pass over him." The purpose of the angelic curse is "to the end that the living may know that the Most High rules the kingdom of men and gives it to whom he will and sets over it the lowliest of men" (v. 17).[34]

The king was afraid that the dream predicted the loss of his prosperity, and Daniel was afraid because he had to say, "It is you, O king" (Dan. 4:22). The dream revealed "a decree of the Most High . . . that you shall be driven from among men, and your dwelling shall be with the beasts of the field" (vv. 24–25). The stump of the tree, under God's sovereign direction, would be restored to Nebuchadnezzar when he lifted his eyes to heaven out of an acceptance of the Most High's dominion (v. 25). "Therefore, O king, . . . break off your sins by practicing righteousness, and your iniquities by showing mercy to the oppressed, that there

---

34. Norman Porteous observes: "Nebuchadnezzar must first learn humility before he can make the general truth of God's sovereignty truly his own. . . . That God can set up in a position of power the lowliest of men is a commonplace of Scripture (see Job 5:11; the Song of Hannah; 1 Sam. 2:7–8; Ps. 113:7–8; the Magnificat; Luke 1:52). . . . In Hebrew tradition Joseph was a shining example of this." *Daniel: A Commentary,* OTL (Philadelphia: Westminster, 1965), 69.

may perhaps be a lengthening of your prosperity" (v. 27). As we have seen in this discussion, godly leaders are characterized by a dependence upon God's sovereign providence, enabling their character to radiate humility in extending grace and mercy to the oppressed.

At the end of twelve months, Nebuchadnezzar was walking on the roof of his palace, filled with a sense of his own grandeur. "Is not this great Babylon, which I have built by my mighty power as a royal residence and for the glory of my majesty?" (Dan. 4:30). Immediately a voice from heaven executed the watchman's threat, and the king became animal-like in his mind and behavior. We can discern three important truths from this sin and its consequence. First, the foundational sin was hubris, an overweening sense of self that blinds us to the presence of God. Second, pride brings a form of insanity as its consequence. Perhaps we may refer to this as a sense of superiority to human laws and life—a sense that we are above God's will for his creation. Some scholars have referred to the king's insanity as boanthropy, a disease in which a person takes on the mental and physical characteristics of an animal. Perhaps in Nebuchadnezzar's case boanthropy was the curse. But a prideful person ordinarily experiences a loss of perspective that exposes an intoxicating loss of reality in the delusional grandeur of oneself. Third, the primal sin of pride undermines the order of creation as established by the image of God in humanity (Gen. 1:26–28). It moves a person from vice-regency under God to a rule as a self-imposed god against God. Instead of elevating his God-given gifts, the person becomes beastly in mind and behavior, devoid of the goodness that the Creator ordained. In the language of Ezekiel, Isaiah, and Daniel, he embarks on the way of death rather than the pleasures of godly living. He trades his sense of the grandeur of God for the delusion of his own might and majesty.

When Nebuchadnezzar "lifted [his] eyes to heaven" (Dan.

4:34), his wisdom was restored, his perspective was clarified, and the effectiveness of his leadership returned. He then stated, "I praise and exalt and glorify the King of heaven, because everything he does is right and all his ways are just. And those who walk in pride he is able to humble" (4:37, NIV). God's humiliation of pride is a blessing, and his exaltation of humility is an encouraging guidepost of godly living.

The Kings' Lessons for Us

Throughout these descriptions of idolatrous kings, the arrogance of highly placed—and condemned—people has been an underlying tension. What about me? I am not a king nor do I claim to be God in my daily life. Could it be that the kings of Tyre and Babylon were exemplars of sinful humanity—in particular the powerful empires that they represented? If the cities were condemned, were not the people as guilty as the king in their idolatrous ways? Daniel 3 teaches this in an undeniable way. There were only three exceptions to the idolatrous worship on the plain of Dura. Throughout the Bible we are warned that arrogance applies to all sinners, and their ultimate punishment—namely death—is the human condition. So yes, the kings offer a glimpse into our hearts as well. E. J. Young expressed this well: "Isaiah wisely uses this strong language that we may ponder our own condition, and align ourselves not with those whose doom is sure but with Him in whose hand is all power and strength."[35] Pride can occur not merely in bombastic speech or a haughty demeanor but also in a failure to acknowledge God's presence and providence in the circumstances of life. When people ignore God in favor of their own wisdom and

---

35. Young, *The Book of Isaiah*, 1:439. Also, "Thus these dealings of God with the great monarch are lessons for all persons in all periods." G. H. Lang, *The Histories and Prophecies of Daniel* (Grand Rapids: Kregel, 1940), 64.

accomplishments, they make themselves gods in their personal palaces, without care or concern for God's glory or the people suffering around them.

American believers should be very cautious, because their culture is widely acknowledged to be Babylonian in its current condition. Meg Greenfield, former editorialist for *Newsweek*, noted in 1993:

> What makes it so hard for a president to stay human is the way people treat him the minute he ascends to office. He is spoiled. He is revered. He is granted an incredible amount of power, not of the practical political kind so much as the power to make his immediate personal convenience and interest override those of everyone else in the room or the building or the city.[36]

Nancy Gibbs similarly observed, "Self-aggrandizement has become both fashionable and fashion. . . . The problems we face are too fierce to accommodate arrogance."[37] In a later article she wrote,

> Powerful men . . . tend to be risk takers or at least assess risk differently—as do narcissists who come to believe that ordinary rules don't apply. They are often surrounded by enablers with a personal and political interest in protecting them to the point of covering up their follies, indiscretions and crimes.[38]

In a word, the enemy surrounds us. Pride is resident in our hearts because we are sinners, and it collectively saturates our culture, which honors accomplished people as heroic gods.

---

36. Meg Greenfield, "Staying Human," *Newsweek* (February 1, 1993), 76.

37. Nancy Gibbs, "The Age of Arrogance," *Time* (November 8, 2009), 64.

38. Nancy Gibbs, "Men Behaving Badly: What Is It about Power That Makes Men Crazy?," *Time* (May 20, 2011), 27.

Once again we have seen that pride is self-centered in contrast to humility, which is God-centered. We must not forget that in the dark valleys of presumptuous kings are the bright lights of Ezekiels, Isaiahs, and Daniels. The words of Paul bring their godliness to bear on our lives: "Look carefully then how you walk, not as unwise but as wise, making the best use of the time, because the days are evil" (Eph. 5:15–16).

Summary

The prophets vividly portrayed the Lord's humiliation of proud rulers who "fell" spectacularly to their deaths. God intervened in the histories of Mesopotamia, Egypt, and Tyre "so that they will know that I am the LORD" of creation. Ezekiel recorded that Tyre's economic power led its rulers to delusional claims of deity. Isaiah taunted the king of Babylon, the archetypal representative of imperial pride. Ezekiel particularly recalled Eden, where the traitorous cherub infected arrogant leaders with an insatiable desire to play God. Humanity has followed the proud rulers without missing a beat. Nebuchadnezzar illustrated a mighty king who was transformed from persecutor of God's people to proclaimer of God's dominion over the earth.

Key Terms

chaos. The effect of sin on the orders of creation as represented biblically by dragons and monsters (Leviathan).
cherub. Angelic guardians of God's glory (cf. Ezek. 1; 10).
Day Star. A title of a king who is believed to be the hope of the world (cf. Acts 12:21–23).
divine assembly. In the ancient world, pagan religions believed in an assembly of gods who would determine the affairs of the world.

gates. Passageways for transportation and trade.

heart. The center or identity of the person.

hubris. An exaggerated sense of self, generally synonymous with pride.

ignominious. Disgraceful, humiliating.

insolence. Rudeness, impudence.

invincibility. Incapable of being defeated.

king. In the ancient world, beyond an individual ruler, a corporate representative of the people who is accountable to God.

Most High. A title for God that exalts him as greater than everything.

mountains, seas. As metaphors, the dwelling places of the gods.

pompous. High-sounding, bombastic words and behavior to parade one's self-importance.

presumptuous. Arrogant attitude or behavior.

prototypical. An original example on which later examples are based or judged.

Shaddai. God Almighty as sovereign of the earth.

Questions for Discussion

1. How do the times of the prophets with their international upheavals parallel our own?
2. Why are economic power and strong defenses inadequate for security in this world?
3. Who governs the affairs of nations (cf. Acts 17:24–26)?
4. Do the oracles against the nations in the Prophets demonstrate that only empires will be judged?
5. Why does Isaiah 14 refer to the king of Babylon rather than to Satan, even though we can be sure that Satan was the tempter of the king?
6. Why do you think that the historical Babylon is presented as "mystery Babylon" in Revelation 17 and 18?

7. Do you think that the Bible intends for us to see ourselves in the folly of ancient rulers? Should we carefully note that timeless truths are often communicated indirectly across the ages?

For Further Reading

Shuster, Marguerite. *The Fall and Sin: What We Have Become as Sinners*. Grand Rapids: Eerdmans, 2004. A very fine supplement for our concerns. Her third chapter discusses "The Fall as Pride and Unbelief."

5

The Great Reversal
in the Gospels

RECENTLY THE "I Am the Greatest" icon, Muhammed Ali, passed away, leaving a long list of tributes from his admirers. Cassius Clay became Muhammed Ali through one of the most controversial yet innovative centuries of history. On June 5, 2016, *The Washington Post* eulogized that Ali "declared himself 'the greatest' and proved it with his fists . . . and who transcended the world of sports to become a symbol of the antiwar movement of the 1960s and a global ambassador for cross-cultural understanding."[1] Ali carried numerous titles besides heavyweight champion of the world: "a citizen of the world," "The Louisville Lip," "The Greatest of All Time," "The Peoples' Champion," and "The Greatest. Period." *Time* similarly stated, "We made him a

---

1. Matt Schudel and Bart Barnes, "Muhammed Ali, Boxing Icon and Global Goodwill Ambassador, Dies at 74," *The Washington Times*, June 4, 2016, https://www.washingtonpost.com/sports/muhammad-ali-boxing-champion-and-global-good-will-ambassador-dies-at-74/2016/06/04/cc3dc3bc-29c3-11e6-ae4a-3cdd5fe74204_story.html?utm_term=.c335f44a46bd.

symbol of the resistance to war, of the racial struggle, and of the individual standing up to establishment pressure."[2] The point of interest here: Muhammed Ali's global acclaim highlights that our world is yearning for genuine, nontransitory significance. The frustration is so deep that people feel that greatness can only be attained by bravado and violence. Has this not always been the case? The exception was Jesus, "who for the joy that was set before him endured the cross, despising the shame, and is seated at the right hand of the throne of God" (Heb. 12:2). These are very different perceptions of greatness! Which, we wonder, is truly great? The answer to this question is our present concern and carries with it the difference between the way the world works and the way of biblical wisdom.

As the disciples and Jesus turned toward Jerusalem, the disciples were deeply concerned with their own greatness; namely, their personal importance and potential leadership positions in Jesus' kingdom. This may be our concern as well, because we all want to live significantly in our relatively short time on this earth. Jesus corrected their misguided expectation by saying that "whoever humbles himself like this child is the greatest in the kingdom of heaven" (Matt. 18:4; cf. 20:27; Mark 9:36–37; 10:43–44; Luke 18:17; 22:26). Greatness in Christ's kingdom somehow involves a childlike humility in devotion to the Lord. What does this mean for the apostles and us?

Jesus moved the counterintuitive reversal of values in Proverb's "way of wisdom" to the center of his kingdom's ethical agenda. Its promise saturates the Bible: God humbles the proud and exalts humble believers. In a parable Luke taught that the honored places at a feast were the lowest ones, because "everyone who exalts himself will be humbled, and he who humbles himself will be exalted" (Luke 14:11). Similarly, Jesus rebuked the

2. *Time* (June 20, 2016), 44.

self-righteousness of Pharisees while commending the humility of the publican (Luke 18:14; cf. Matt. 23:12), bypassing the social hierarchy of Jewish leadership.

The principle of humility's greatness had characterized Christ's life from his birth. Elizabeth's blessing (Luke 1:45) was followed by Mary's Magnificat (vv. 46–55). Mary spontaneously sang the same theme Hannah had in 1 Samuel 2:1–10: "For he has been mindful of the humbled state of his servant [in choosing her as the mother of the Lord]. . . . He [the Mighty One] has scattered those who are proud in their innermost thoughts. He has brought down rulers from their thrones and has lifted up the humble." Hannah had said, "The LORD sends poverty and wealth; he humbles and he exalts" (1 Sam. 2:7). Jesus introduced his ministry with a well-known Messianic expectation from Isaiah 61:1–2 and 58:6:

> The Spirit of the Lord is upon me,
>> because he has anointed me
>> to proclaim good news to the poor.
>
> He has sent me to proclaim liberty to the captives
>> and recovering of sight to the blind,
>> to set at liberty those who are oppressed. (Luke 4:18)

The theme of humility as service to the lowly and needy in society is the tapestry that frames Jesus' teaching on pride and humility. We will develop these themes on the way to the cross through Christ's use of images and promises from Old Testament wisdom. His disciples are instructed to seek greatness in the eyes of God by:

- Being willing to become childlike under God,
- Being willing to be last for God,

- Being willing to serve all people for God, and
- Being willing to follow Christ on the road to Calvary.

These emphases are aspects of a single biblical concept of godly humility. They reflect the conviction that a follower of Christ should live confident that God will exalt humble believers in his time and way. We will define the concept through the lens of the dispute about greatness in the parallel passages (Matt. 18; Mark 9; Luke 9), then introduce related passages and conclude with the Lord's example as he washed his disciples' feet and "gave his life as a ransom for many."[3]

The setting of the discussion about godly greatness occurs in Jesus' announcement of his passion and its implications for the disciples' character.[4] The Master and his disciples were in Galilee, preparing for "the way" to Jerusalem to face the entrenched opposition of Jewish authorities. Central passages on kingdom greatness follow Peter's confession, which affirmed Christ as the anticipated Messiah and Son of the Living God (Matt. 16:13–20; cf. 9:27–30; Luke 8:18–27). The Transfiguration was validated by the Father and witnessed by Peter, James, and John. Luke 9:46–48, like parallel passages in Matthew 18 and Mark 9, focuses on Jesus' determination to go to Jerusalem, which provoked fear in the disciples.[5] Had they misunderstood his identity as a king

---

3. Though parallel, the Synoptics present Jesus' mandate for humility with distinctive emphases. Matthew 18:3–5 calls for a transformation from self-centered concerns about greatness to a childlike powerlessness to be counted as great. Mark and Luke emphasize that humility involves serving all people in Jesus' name, which includes the reception of the Father as well. Luke closes his pericope stating that even "the least among you all is great," meaning that all people are to be served as God's creation. All of the accounts agree that humility is measured by loving service of the lowly, who are otherwise neglected and oppressed in prideful relationships.

4. Michael Wilkins makes the helpful point that Matthew portrays the disciples in positive and negative ways so that they can be examples for us. Their struggles in following Jesus are ours as well. *Discipleship in the Ancient World and Matthew's Gospel*, 2nd ed. (Grand Rapids: Baker Books, 1995), 169.

5. In Luke the question of greatness occurs between Jesus' announcement of his

and the anticipation of a kingdom? The context was a confusing juxtaposition between suffering and glory, between lowliness and royalty. According to the Synoptics, they "were afraid to ask him" for further information about the distressing news. "But they did not understand the saying, and were afraid to ask him" (Mark 9:32).[6]

Like Mark, Luke developed "the way" theme, apparently influenced by Isaiah 50:7–9, where the Servant of Yahweh "set [his] face like flint," knowing that he would be vindicated rather than shamed. The underlying idea was that discipleship is a way of suffering. As the final journey began, the question of greatness arose for the first time in Luke. The impulse of the apostles to enhance their prestige in the kingdom was directly at odds with the self-sacrificing standard of their Lord. In the words of Leon Morris, "Jesus had just spoken of his sacrificial death for sinners. They were speaking of their pride of place."[7] They simply had not understood the Scriptures or the ways of God. "O foolish ones, and slow of heart to believe all that the prophets have spoken! Was it not necessary that the Christ should suffer these things and enter into his glory?" (Luke 24:25–26).

The dispute about greatness is also a sequel in Matthew ("at that time") to Peter's inquiry about the temple tax (Matt. 17:24–27). Ἐν ἐκείνῃ τῇ ὥρᾳ is a temporal link, and was frequently used by Matthew to suggest interrupted flow in the narrative (cf. 3:1; 12:1; 14:1). Peter had encountered collectors of the half-shekel toll and responded to their question regarding if

---

death (9:44–45) and the commencement of the final journey to Jerusalem (9:51).

6. "Their sheepish silence shows that the disciples knew that Jesus would not approve of their conversation and motives behind it." Craig Evans, *Mark 8:27–16:20*, vol. WBC 34B (Nashville: Nelson, 2001), 61.

7. Leon Morris, *Luke: An Introduction and Commentary* (Grand Rapids: Eerdmans, 1988), 192. Adele Yarbro Collins suggests that the disciples do not wish to hear anything further of the suffering of the Son of Man and do not wish to suffer themselves, so here each wants not only to be great, but to be greater than the others. *Mark: A Commentary*, Hermeneia (New York: Doubleday, 2007), 444.

his teacher paid the tax. When Peter returned, Jesus asked him about the source of revenues for kings' treasuries—did it come from their sons or others? "From others," Peter replied. Jesus then concluded, "Then the sons are free" (Matt. 17:26). To avoid offense, he instructed Peter to pay a shekel for both of them. The miraculous coin in the fish's mouth indicated the humility of submission to taxation—a vocational responsibility in Peter's fishing—even though the King is the master of all creation. This episode may seem unrelated to us in our modern setting, but in the Gospel setting it demonstrated that God-honoring humility extends to every area of life. The disciples understood their sonship under Christ and were pressing the implication of royalty for their status in his kingdom. The connection suggests a contrast between "kings of the earth" and the sons of a very different kingdom. Too frequently the distinction is ignored because, like Israel, we want to be "like the nations" with a share of their ostentatious power.

Being Willing to Become Childlike under God

Matthew bases Jesus' view of greatness on a question of the disciples, "Who is the greatest in the kingdom of heaven?" (18:1).[8] The principle, in turn, connects various teachings about ethics in his kingdom. Ulrich Luz makes Jesus' response about childlikeness (vv. 2–4) the foundational principle of relationships among his followers. "I read it then as a kind of statement of

8. In Luke 9:46–48 διαλογισμὸς should be translated "argument," showing that their pride was evident in their concern and that Jesus, at the same time, was "knowing their thoughts" (NIV). The point is profound, because all sinners want to think that they are the greatest! From the fall in Genesis 3, this is the easily besetting sin of humanity. Alfred Plummer observes, "The point in dispute was, who among themselves was greater than the rest of them; who stood nearest to the Christ, and had the highest place in the Kingdom (Mt.). . . . The thought in their hearts was, Am not I the greatest?" *A Critical and Exegetical Commentary on the Gospel of Luke*, 5th ed., ICC (Edinburgh: T&T Clark, 1922), 257.

principle that is important for the entire discourse."⁹ Its threefold repetition in 18:1–5; 20:20–28; and 23:8–12 supports Luz's point. In brief, the willingness to live humbly in service to God and others is the defining characteristic of greatness in the kingdom of heaven.

Jesus' answer involved the connection of humility with character and acceptance of children, who were referred to as παιδία (Matt. 18:2–5) and μικροί (vv. 6–14). Μέγας ("great") suggests position and honor, so that "the greatest" would be the most outstanding leader whose position would give them status and prestige. Jesus introduced his answer by summoning a child, whom he placed in their midst, apparently as a rabbinic gesture for instruction (v. 2).[10] He used the child to personalize his ethical principle as a challenge to the disciples, "Truly, I say to you, unless you turn and become like children, you will never enter the kingdom of heaven" (v. 3). The Talmud notes that rabbis at the time thought that instruction of children under twelve years of age was considered wasted time.[11] Mark noted that Jesus placed the child in their midst and then held him. Thus, Jesus affirmed that the child was old enough to understand and young enough to be held—a small child who would exemplify humility in serving the helpless people.

What does this mean? "Kingdom of heaven" is used in this context of ethical criteria rather than earthly standards. It is a new order of righteousness and wisdom, which conforms to Jesus' "humility in heart" (Matt. 11:19). If entry into the kingdom of heaven is at stake, then how does a person become a child again after becoming an adult? The criterion and its interpretation are impossible physically. Thus the criterion leads us in

9. Ibid., 424.
10. Children were often brought to rabbis and prominent teachers to be blessed by the laying on of hands. When he sat down, Jesus underscored his authority as a teacher.
11. *TDNT*, s.v. "παῖς," by Albrecht Oepke, 5:646.

the direction of a fundamental change in spiritual maturity.[12] This maturation in 18:3 refers to a countercultural reversal from prevailing standards of thought and behavior. Darrell Bock correctly emphasizes, "To receive God enhances the value of other persons. Jesus is calling on the disciples to change the way they see people: be kind to the 'lowly,' act in a way that ignores status."[13]

How does childlikeness define Jesus' understanding of pride and humility? Participation in Jesus' kingdom requires an ethical transformation from conventional standards like position, power, and prestige.[14] The criterion for greatness is not status markers like these, and the mandate to become like a child is extraordinary in worldly terms. This is reflected in a later episode. Children were brought to Jesus "so that he might lay his hands on them and pray" (Matt 19:13). The disciples tried to intervene and somehow prevent the blessing. But Jesus responded, "Let the little children come to me and do not hinder them, for to such belongs the kingdom of heaven" (v. 14). As in chapter 18, "such ones" (τοιούτων) indicates not only the small children that he blessed but also believers who follow him by maturing to be poor in spirit and humble as a child.

Scholars have speculated about the meaning of childhood as a role model for discipleship. Interpreters have tended to read into the requirement their own understanding of what a child should be; namely, the disciples should exemplify compliant, well-mannered followers since ideal children would not be quarrelsome. Obviously, children can be the opposite of ideal, which is why biblical wisdom counsels discipline and training. Two

12. The verb for "turn" (στραφῆτε) does not mean a literal return to childhood, but rather a change in conduct: a rejection of both pretension and concern for worldly prestige.
13. Darrell Bock, *Luke 1:1–9:50*, 2 vols., BECNT (Grand Rapids: Baker Academic, 1994), 1.896.
14. "True greatness is not earthly greatness but its opposite." Morris, *Luke*, 192.

[handwritten margin note: Reached = ptoochos + dependence]

textual connections will guide us toward a more appropriate meaning of the image. First, Robert Gundry observed that Jesus' summons used the same verb (προσκαλέω) that was used with the calling of the disciples, because "from the very beginning the child stands for a disciple and Matthew's word clearly indicates the summoning of the disciples in 10:1; 15:32; 20:25."[15] Following Christ means that one must be like a child.

Second, if biblical humility does not mean mere compliance, Matthew 18:4 suggests an added dimension: "whoever humbles himself like this child is the greatest in the kingdom of heaven." The child/disciple must be characterized by humility, and greatness—according to Jesus—means self-humiliation to a childlikeness; namely, a conscious self-willing to serve God whatever that may involve. The Greek descriptive ταπεινός primarily means humility in the sense of lowliness; a lowly person is willing to be powerless and insignificant—a poverty in status, and perhaps circumstances, for the sake of the Master.[16] This is tantamount to saying that they are willing to live for the glory of God rather than for themselves.

The implication of powerlessness and dependence aligns with the Old Testament emphasis discussed in earlier chapters. In the Psalms and Prophets, we may recall, wicked people opposed powerless believers as a way of gaining wealth. The arrogant wicked wore pride as their necklace and violence covered them like a garment (Ps. 73:6). Humble believers, on the

---

15. Robert Gundry, *Matthew: A Commentary on His Handbook for a Mixed Church under Persecution*, 2nd ed. (Grand Rapids: Eerdmans, 1994), 360.

16. Matthew 11:16–25 suggests that a humble person will be receptive to God's revelation and his prophets, while pride will be arrogantly hostile to God's word and prophets. Nevertheless, wisdom has been vindicated by the righteousness of faith in God's truth. This truth had been manifested in John's austere call for repentance, and Jesus coming to save sinners, yet the pride of "this generation" rejected both. Similar in emphasis is Acts 4:13: "When they saw the courage of Peter and John and realized that they were unschooled, ordinary men, they were astonished and they took note that these men had been with Jesus" (NIV).

other hand, cried out to God as their refuge and hope. Their dependence on the Lord for their needs was a childlike cry for deliverance. Jesus clearly seems to be using that background to instruct his followers in general and the apostles in particular. He counsels contentment with a childlike status in his kingdom. This added a Trinitarian dimension to his mandate; *child* is a familial analogy, suggesting Jesus' dependence on the Father even as his followers become humble as they follow the Son in dependence on the Father. Thus, humility becomes a family trait of filial devotion rather than a more vague humiliation for the sake of future rewards. Matthew 18:5 draws this implication: "Whoever receives one such child in my name receives me, but whoever causes one of these little ones who believe in me to sin, it would be better for him . . . to be drowned in the depth of the sea" (cf. Mark 9:37, Luke 9:48). "In my name" points to a humility that accepts any believer regardless of circumstances or social advantage—simply because of a relationship that is based on mutual commitment to Christ. It means an embrace of suffering and death if necessary.

Humility thus becomes the distinguishing characteristic of the messianic community. It requires a willingness to change one's orientation from self-promotion to a recognition of one's need for mutual relationships with other believers and the Trinity's mission to the world.[17] In Matthew 18, Jesus reminds his disciples of their forgiveness as a platform for living in a forgiving way in the family of God. Jesus as Messiah occupies the center of the chapter as the one who is present among his followers, even if only two or three are gathered together

---

17. "I would suggest that . . . most of the teaching can be subsumed under the rubric of humility: humility with regard to one's own place in the kingdom, receiving rather than despising Jesus' little ones, administering and accepting correction, and willingness to forgive others." Don Garlington, "Who Is the Greatest?," *JETS* 53 (June 2010): 290.

(vv. 19–20). Matthew's readers knew that Jesus had to go the city of suffering, the persecutor of prophets (16:21; cf. 20:17, 19), and geographical markers in 20:17, 29 indicated that he would soon join the parade of martyrs.

The notion of sacrificial commitment is similar to Matthew 5:3, where the "poor in spirit" participate in the kingdom of heaven—a passage where distinction in rank is affirmed (vv. 19–20). It also emphasizes the close connection between Jesus' ethical instruction and the Old Testament. According to David Hill:

> The "poor in spirit" are neither the "poor in courage" (i.e., in "spiritedness") nor "in the Holy Spirit," nor "in spiritual awareness"; they are the *nāwîm* of the OT (LXX *ptōchoi*)—those who, because of long economic and social distress, have confidence only in God.... The term had a clear religious connotation: the poor and afflicted saints of God (cf. Ps. Sol. 10:7). '*Anî.* '*ānāw,* and '*ebyôn* are synonyms for this attitude of heart and mind, and the Greek *ptōchos* and *praüs* (which translates '*ānî* and '*ānāw* at Zech. 9:9 and Ps. 25 (24), 9) cannot easily be distinguished. The phrase "poor in spirit" is the exact equivalent of '*nwy rwh* in 1QM xiv.7 (cf. *rwh 'nwh* in 1QS iv.3), which denotes "the humble poor who trust in God's help."[18]

In biblical anthropology the term *spirit* reflects willing dependence on God and an awareness of one's need for his enablement and provision.[19] God's "little ones" (ἕνα τῶν μικρῶν in Matt. 18:6, 10, 14) are those who are willing to choose the significance of God and his people and avoid the self-centered ambitions of

---

18. David Hill, *The Gospel of Matthew*, New Century Bible (London: Marshall, Morgan & Scott, 1972), 10.

19. Hans Walter Wolff, *Anthropology of the Old Testament*, trans. Margaret Kohl (Philadelphia: Fortress, 1974), 37–39.

the world. They are promised God's presence and protection. In a contrary way, judgment will be meted out to their worldly seducers. Lux reads the reflexive self-humiliation as a way of life, including attitude and behavior:

> While the disciples' lowliness *also* includes the attitude of humility, it involves much more than an inner stance. One must work at the practice of lowliness. It is expressed, for example, by extending hospitality to children (v. 5), by loving "little ones" as brothers and sisters (vv. 10–14), by being willing to forgive without limitations (vv. 21–22), by giving up one's own possessions out of love for one's neighbor (19:16–21), and above all by renouncing hierarchical honors (23:8–10) by serving (20:26–28; 23:11).[20]

Therefore, this kind of humility becomes the foundation of a loving, godly community that should characterize the church.

Sacrificial willingness to follow the Master in the lowliness of humility is introduced in Matthew 10:34–39 with an undertone of entering a path of suffering, if necessary. "And whoever does not take his cross and follow me is not worthy of me. Whoever finds his life will lose it, and whoever loses his life for my sake will find it" (cf. Mark 8:34–35; Luke 9:23–24). Matthew 16:24–28 made the same point about taking up one's cross to save one's life and added that "the Son of Man is going to come with his angels in the glory of his Father, and then he will repay each person according to what he has done" (v. 27). In the case of Christ, the sacrifice was evident in his messianic service and atoning payment for the salvation of his people. In the case of his followers, the humility of sacrificing one's own interests for the Lord and his people demands a passionate commitment

20. Ulrich Luz, *Matthew 18–20: A Commentary*, trans. James Crouch, Hermeneia (Minneapolis: Augsburg Fortress, 2005), 429.

to God-centeredness, a lowliness that chooses service over the world's alluring temptations.

In 18:5 Matthew referred to "one such child [ἕνα τῶν μικρῶν τούτον] in my name receiv[ing] me." This shows a shift from being childlike in character to embracing (rather than rejecting) a lowly person. Receiving children literally, who have nothing to give in return, is an indication of a person's humility that does not use personal power and prestige as the criterion of fellowship in community. "Such little ones" encompasses all lowly ones who are received by the Lord in spite of their social unimportance. The implication is that Jesus' instruction on humility has both personal and social nuances; it is a personal mandate with the consequence of social unity. Matthew summoned Jesus' disciples to behavior that expressed his concern about unity and community among Christ's followers—unity that was shredded by competitive ambition to be "great." His teaching about humility prohibited comparisons between believers, because they are inevitably followed by competition. John warned his churches to have nothing to do with Diotrephes, "who likes to put himself first, does not acknowledge our authority. . . . talking wicked nonsense against us" (3 John 9–10). By taking the child to himself, Jesus exemplified God's view of greatness that gives all glory to the Godhead rather than the self.[21] How we receive others is a test of our greater love of God.

Being Willing to Be Last for God

Later in Matthew Jesus expanded on the godliness of humility by commenting on a "rich young ruler," who had left Jesus while grieving because he had many possessions: "It is easier for a camel to go through the eye of a needle than for a rich person to

---

21. In other words, if Jesus is a child/servant who humbly accepted the mission of his Father, then his disciples are expected to follow his example.

enter the kingdom of God" (19:24). The disciples, still struggling with the reversal of values, asked, "Who then can be saved?" (v. 25). They had left everything to follow him, so what will they gain for their sacrificial commitment? Jesus' answer was that "there is only One who is good . . . but with God [by grace] all things are possible" (vv. 17, 26). One cannot interpret life apart from God as people are prone to do. Those who have sacrificially followed him in faith "will receive a hundredfold and will inherit eternal life." The idea is that a progressive release of one's worldly pride will allow God to graciously live through them. This will result in an ultimate reversal of position. "Many who are first will be last, and the last first" (v. 30). God's enabling presence is experienced in the Spirit. Here the "kingdom" blends the ethical realm with eschatological promise. Those who sacrificially follow the example of their Master live a countercultural life in the world, in contrast to the arrogant rulers of worldly kingdoms. People who have a sense of how lost they are apart from God are more likely to hear these hard teachings than those who are satisfied with their condition in life.

The stunning principle of the countercultural emphasis is that "many who are first will be last, and the last first" (Matt. 19:30; Mark 10:31; Luke 13:30). The oft-repeated promise is embedded with the childlike standard in Mark 9:33–36 (cf. 10:31), meaning that related terms in the passage like "child" and "youngest" (Luke 22:26) and "last," "least," and "slave" probably would share similar meanings. In Evans's words, "One who desires to be first must be a servant, and that means service to the least powerful and least influential such as children."[22]

To begin with, at least three possible misunderstandings must be dismissed. First, Jesus was not teaching that greatness in his kingdom is poverty in this life. He was not advocating a

22. Evans, *Mark 8:27–16:20*, 61.

"vow of poverty." To be willing to be poor in the Master's service is not the same as a necessity to live in poverty. God's grace and our faith cannot be removed from the principle (cf. Matt 20:1–16, esp. v. 16). Second, Jesus was not teaching an automatic reversal of rank and roles in heaven and on earth. No biblical law necessitates the rule of poor and oppressed people over their rich and powerful counterparts. The "rich young ruler" is an example of those who may be ultimately last, but his lack of dedication was the issue rather than his wealth. Clearly, however, an "abundance of possessions" can promote "all kinds of greed" (Luke 12:13–20). By the same token, the humble "great" are first, because they are "rich toward God" and "served a single Master" (16:13–15; cf. 12:21). Third, "first and last" does not mean that seniority as a disciple means greatness in community. Judas Iscariot was one of the first disciples, but he was "doomed to destruction" (John 17:12). Paul was the last of the apostles (1 Cor. 15:8–9), but he exemplified lowly zeal for God's glory (2 Cor. 11:23). God's measure of greatness is the opposite of worldly standards. "God knows your hearts. For what is exalted among men is an abomination in the sight of God" (Luke 16:15).

The terminology of the reversal reaffirms the countercultural emphasis. "Child" or "the youngest," as we have seen, meant a willingness to be powerless or insignificant in the service of the Master. "Last" translates ἔσχατος, meaning last in rank (1 Cor. 4:9), last in time ("the last days," John 6:39, *passim*), or uttermost (Acts 1:8). Ethically, it denotes "the least honorable" as the opposite of πρῶτος ("first," Mark 9:35; 10:44). Thus, it denotes extremity, or a willingness to be lowest in rank. "Least" (ἐλάχιστος) is an adjectival superlative of μικρός (cf. Matt 18:6), indicating a willingness to serve "the least of these my brethren (Matt 25:40; cf. 1 Cor. 15:9).

The willingness to choose "the lowest place" is illustrated by Jesus' parable of the prominent Pharisee's wedding feast

(Luke 14:1–14). He instructed the disciples not to take "the place of honor," lest they be humiliated by having to move for more important guests. If they chose the least important place, they might be honored by a better place in front of their fellow guests. Humility leads to honor rather than shame.[23] To the Pharisee, he counseled invitations to "the poor, crippled, lame, and blind" instead of rich family members and friends for favor with God rather than people. Later in Luke 22:24–30 Jesus used hospitality again to show that the one who serves is greater than those who are seated, "I am among you as the one who serves" (v 27).[24]

The reason that believers should choose sacrifice and suffering for the Lord, if necessary, is the oft-repeated biblical principle of greatness and significance: "everyone who exalts himself will be humbled, and he who humbles himself will be exalted" (Luke 14:11). The principle distinctively emphasized the role of God in the counterintuitive reversal of values; namely, God exalts humble believers who trust him for life and humiliates proud oppressors (Prov. 3:34–35; 11:2; 13:10; 15:25–33; 16:18). It is the biblical "way of wisdom" in which pride falls because it focuses on self-interest and ignores God-honoring service for other people. Pride motivates friendship with the world and enmity toward God (James 4:4–6; 1 John 2:15–17). But God gives more grace to the humble who submit themselves to the Spirit and one another (cf. 1 Peter 5:5–6). Only God can penetrate and transform our deeply ingrained pride.

Humility was exemplified by Joseph, Daniel, and the apostles. Pride was exemplified by the Pharisees. They placed heavy

23. Public shame and loss of face was a humiliation to be avoided at all costs. In the parable humility offered the social advantage of possible honor with a higher place (cf. R. Akiba, *Leviticus Rabbah* 1.5).

24. James 2:5–7 (NIV) condemns favoritism with the words, "Has not God chosen those who are poor in the eyes of the world to be rich in faith and to inherit the kingdom he promised to those who love him?"

burdens on peoples' shoulders (Matt. 23:3), in contrast to Jesus' heart of humility and gentleness with a light burden (11:29–30). They loved places of honor and lofty titles. They looked "beautiful on the outside but on the inside were full of the bones of the dead" (23:27, NIV). Even the tax collector in the parable was justified before God ahead of the Pharisee, because "everyone who exalts himself will be humbled, and he who humbles himself will be exalted" (Luke 14:11; cf. Matt 23:12).

I have seen this promise personally from my involvement for forty-three years in India. The ministry is among the Dalit, the untouchable poor. These Christians have little to offer except their dedication to the work of the Lord among people that the elites have enslaved. Over time God has used them to bring thousands to himself. He has blessed them with skills to lead in their hospital, orphanage, secondary school, and seminary. You will not find more than a modicum of pride among these people. I say this because all people struggle with pride, but they are extremely humble in the opinion of Western visitors. They don't parade their humility either, because they are living out "a God thing" in a desperately poor place. By being faithful among the lowly, they have found the blessings of being first and great by the grace of God. This is how the promise works in the present, and it will reach its fullness in the future.

In summary, God's servants are great because they are willing to be last for God and his people. They do not allow pride to blind them to the need for trusting God in the circumstances of life. They are willing to serve one another, even if the needy ones among them are not able to repay their kindness. They know that God will reward them in his time. And they embrace a humble lifestyle not from a sense of grudging obligation but rather from a loving commitment to the Master in the Spirit. Worldly pride is the opposite. It defines greatness as self-glorification by striving for power and prestige at the expense of others.

Being Willing to Serve All People for God

In Mark 9:35 and 10:43 Jesus correlates childlikeness with a willingness to be a servant (διάκονος or "slave," δοῦλος) of all. Again, "child," "last," and "slave" share our central passage on humility and define biblical greatness as a willingness to be powerless in status, the least in rank, and in the service of all for the Master. Explicit obedience to the Lord's example was the consistent standard, and this passage transitions this chapter from the teaching of Jesus to his example for believers. The criterion of humility as service is intensified in Jesus' declaration, "Whoever would be great among you must be your servant, and whoever would be first among you must be slave of all" (vv. 43–44). France observed, "The only new term introduced here is δοῦλος, a further extension of subjection, since a δοῦλος had far less self-determination even than a διάκονος . . . it is to *everyone* (πάντων) that precedence must be given."[25]

James and John came to him and expressed a desire for him "to do for us whatever we ask" (Mark 10:35). They requested honored places in his impending kingdom: "Grant us to sit, one at your right hand and one at your left, in your glory" (v. 37). The seat on the right may have been the most prestigious, but with the king on his throne, courtiers on both sides would have highest honors.[26] Interestingly, Peter had taken the initiative in verse 28, but now the brothers' request would leave no place for

25. R. T. France, *The Gospel of Mark*, New International Greek Testament Commentary (Grand Rapids: Eerdmans, 2002), 419.

26. According to Matthew 20:20–21, the mother of the brothers makes the request. But Jesus understands the source of the request when he replies, "You [plural] do not know what you [plural] are asking." The plural indicates that Jesus was addressing James and John rather than their mother. The reader should not miss the irony that Jesus' victory over sin on the cross—a display of sovereign authority—took place between "two robbers, one on his right and one on his left" amid the derisive insults of the robbers and observers (Mark 15:25–35).

him and the others. The indignation of the other ten disciples indicated that the request was heard by all of them (v. 41). They were angry because the brothers had tried to gain an advantage in competition for the highest places. The governing attitude of everyone was self-centeredness: "We want you to do for us whatever we ask" in a hoped-for kingdom in the imminent future. And in verse 39 "their self-confident reply showed that they had not understood Jesus' meaning."[27] C. S. Lewis is insightful when he traces pride to its competitive instinct:

> The point is that each person's pride is in competition with everyone else's pride. . . . Now what you want to get clear is that Pride is *essentially* competitive—is competitive by its very nature—while the other vices are competitive only, so to speak, by accident. Pride gets no pleasure out of having something, only out of having more of it than the next man.[28]

The disciples expressed their pride in terms of honored positions. But they could have sought honor as well through wealth, winning, impressive appearance, or the freedom to unleash injustice, and revenge on hypocritical leaders of the day (cf. Matt. 23). On the other hand, God was present in the Savior who was predicting his vicarious death. That is what made the disciples' concern over their personal greatness so inappropriate. In other words, God's presence removes the question of comparative greatness. In Lewis's words, "If you really get onto any kind of touch with Him you will, in fact, be humble—delightedly humble, feeling the infinite relief of having for once got rid of all the silly nonsense about your own dignity which has made you restless and

27. C. E. B. Cranfield, *The Gospel According to Mark*, The Cambridge Greek Testament Commentary (Cambridge: Cambridge University Press, 1959), 338.

28. C. S. Lewis, *Mere Christianity* (1952; repr., San Francisco: HarperSanFrancisco, 2001), 122.

unhappy all of your life."²⁹ The cautionary lesson for us is that in a day of overwhelming secularity we may have lost "any kind of touch with Him."

Jesus responded that the way to glory in his kingdom involved his "cup" and "baptism" (Mark 10:38); at God's sovereign discretion, the cross must precede the crown. Daniel 7, which backdrops the Markan passage, spoke of a climactic struggle between "the people of the Most High" (v. 18) and the kingdoms of the world. "As for me, Daniel, my thoughts greatly alarmed me, and my color changed" (v. 28). The "cup" of the believer refers to their destined suffering, and the baptism is a metaphor for being immersed in sorrow. Jesus, of course, suffered punishment for sin that was not his, and his vicarious "baptism" was his death that saves those who trust him for their salvation from sin (Mark 10:38). Believers are to suffer. "But if when you do good and suffer for it you endure . . . to this you have been called, because Christ also suffered for you, leaving you an example, so that you might follow in his steps" (1 Peter 2:20–21). Humble service will bring suffering in an arrogant world.³⁰ This inevitable costliness in following Jesus is reviewed in explicit statements like Mark 14:27 and by the likely prospects of their ministries in 13:9–11. It was exemplified by the Messiah himself as he offered his life in willing submission to the Father in the Spirit—but not without the disturbing admission of his misery without consolation (15:34).

The "slave" word group referred to some form of compulsory, dependent service. Biblically, dependence on the Lord was a title of honor and was applied to figures like Moses (Josh. 1:7), Joshua (Judg. 2:8), Abraham (Ps. 105:42), and David (89:3). In Acts 4 it

29. Ibid., 127.

30. "In v. 39 he means by the same terms [as v. 38] simply a sharing in those sufferings which his followers will have to be ready to endure for his sake and which may indeed include martyrdom." Cranfield, *Mark*, 339.

was the descriptive title for David, Jesus ("holy servant"), and believers (4:25, 27, 29). Paul in particular referred to Christians as δοῦλοι of Christ, which made Philemon and Onesimus brothers with precedence over social distinctions (cf. Eph. 6:5–9; Col. 3:22–25). Paul, James, Jude, and Peter used the title of honor in their salutations.

Jesus gathered the disciples to emphasize a truism (οἴδατε) about the abuse of authority by worldly rulers and to sharply distinguish it from his humble leadership (οὐχ οὕτως . . . ὑμῖν). What Jesus commands his disciples "could not possibly be more at odds with conventional wisdom."[31] "Those who are regarded as rulers of Gentiles" refers to imperial power, which was most evident, irrefutable, and visible in its exploitation of all people under its control. Christian servant-leaders, on the other hand, are to be "eager to serve; not lording it over those entrusted to you, but being examples to the flock" under the Chief Shepherd (1 Peter 5:2–3, NIV). Greatness was service, and being first was slavery toward all (Mark 10:44).

"By far the most remarkable and probably disputed saying in Mark follows:"[32] "For even the Son of Man did not come to be served," Jesus emphasized, "but to serve, and to give his life as a ransom for many" (v. 45, NIV). The verse is a complementary synthesis of Daniel 7 and Isaiah 53 that formed Jesus' self-understanding and mission.[33] Three elements of the verse call attention to its extraordinary importance for the topic of humility: the use of "Son of Man" for sacrificial service, the alignment of the "suffering Savior" with Isaiah's servant in chapter 53, and the rare occurrence of "ransom" for his mission. First, Jesus

31. Evans, *Mark 8:27–16:20*, 119.
32. Ibid.
33. Even though Mark's use of Isaiah is not quotably exact, the concentration of vocabulary and thematic coherence suggest that the Servant was to be identified with the "suffering Servant" to come. Cf. W. D. Davies and Dale Allison, *Matthew 19–28* (London: T&T Clark Continuum, 2004), 96.

uses Daniel's title with an ascensive (καί as intensive) force to heighten the difference between the messianic expectation and the reality in Mark: "for even the Son of Man." In Daniel 7:13–14 the Son was given "authority, glory, and sovereign power" in the presence of the everlasting God. This image informed the misunderstanding of the disciples. In a future day of the Lord, imperial authority will be the reality. But the cross must precede the crown, so in the first century sovereignty meant service to conquer sin and the spiritual forces of evil. The disciples needed to understand that a humble servant in submission to God is exercising dominion; this allows the power of God to be manifested through believers.

Second, Jesus aligns his messiahship with the poor, the prisoners, the blind, and the oppressed (Luke 4:18–19, quoting Isa. 61:1–2). He counseled the Pharisee to invite the poor, crippled, and blind to his banquet for the blessing of God (Luke 14:12–14). In Mark 10:45 he identifies himself with the servant in Isaiah 53:1–9:

Who has believed what he has heard from us?
    And to whom has the arm of the LORD been revealed?
For he grew up before him like a young plant,
    and like a root out of dry ground;
he had no form or majesty that we should look at him,
    and no beauty that we should desire him.
He was despised and rejected by men,
    a man of sorrows and acquainted with grief;
and as one from whom men hide their faces
    he was despised, and we esteemed him not.
Surely he has borne our griefs
    and carried our sorrows;
yet we esteemed him stricken,
    smitten by God, and afflicted.

But he was pierced for our transgressions;
    he was crushed for our iniquities;
upon him was the chastisement that brought us peace,
    and with his wounds we are healed.
All we like sheep have gone astray;
    we have turned—every one—to his own way;
and the LORD has laid on him
    the iniquity of us all.
He was oppressed, and he was afflicted,
    yet he opened not his mouth;
like a lamb that is led to the slaughter,
    and like a sheep that before its shearers is silent,
    so he opened not his mouth.
By oppression and judgment he was taken away;
    and as for his generation, who considered
that he was cut off out of the land of the living,
    stricken for the transgression of my people?
And they made his grave with the wicked
    and with a rich man in his death,
although he had done no violence,
    and there was no deceit in his mouth.

The strong language of the passage points not so much to the repulsiveness of the Servant as to his loving identification with his persecuted, believing remnant. He was the epitome of humility and the supreme example of a slave for all. But he was victorious in resurrection, infinitely more than the conquering "rulers of the Gentiles" (Matt. 20:25).

Third, Jesus described his mission to "give his life as a ransom for many" (Mark 10:45). This statement (with its Matthaean parallel) is the only use of λύτρον per se in the New Testament, though cognates are used elsewhere (as in 1 Tim. 2:6). Generally, the term refers to redemptive payments to release people from adverse circumstances such as slavery or imprisonment. Here Mark 10:45 conceptually aligns with Isaiah 53:10–12.[34] The servant was to be sacrificed as a guilt offering (אָשָׁם; cf. Lev. 5:14–6:7; 7:1–7; Num. 5:5–8) to "[bear] the sin of many, and make intercession for the transgressors" (Isa. 53:12). The term *many* apparently is reflected in Mark 10:45. The death of the servant "will justify many, and he will bear their iniquities" (Isa. 53:11, NIV). Though not a quotation, Jesus was willing to sacrifice his life "in place of" (ἀντί) sinners as payment for believers' release from their bondage to sin (Heb. 5:2–3).[35] In brief, he is the greatest, because he was the servant Savior in complete submission to the will of God. Because of his sacrifice, "Therefore I will give him a position among the great, and he will divide the spoils with the strong" (Isa. 53:12, NIV).

Being Willing to Follow Christ on the Road to Calvary

The victory of the Servant is unique, but he left us with a vivid image of our service in John 13:1–17. Just before Passover, Jesus knew that the time had come for him to return to his

34. Ivan Engnell noted that the fourth song (Isa. 52:13–53:12) played an indisputable role in Jesus' self-understanding, in spite of controversies about the passage: "*The chief prophetic line, the messianic line* brought home in Him its last and decisive victory in a revolutionary conception of the *suffering* Messiah, in what is best described as a combination of the 'Ebed Yahweh figure and the idea of the Son of Man. . . . Ch. lii:13–liii:12, the fourth 'Ebed Yahweh song may without any exaggeration be called the most important text of the Old Testament, as it is probably the most often dealt with. . . . It is, further, quite clear also from the emphasis laid here by me so strongly on the fact that 'Ebed Yahweh is none else than the Davidic Messiah himself. This fact is in reality so decisive that it is neither necessary nor possible to indicate more strongly the importance of the foundation in real life that supports the 'Ebed Yahweh messianism, a form of the most central line of faith throughout the history of Israel." "The 'Ebed Yahweh Songs and the Suffering Messiah in 'Deutero-Isaiah,'" *Bulletin of the John Rylands Library* 31 (1948): 54, 73, 93.

35. *TDNT*, s.v. "ἀντί," by Friedrich Buchsel, 1:372–73.

Father. He was aware that "the Father had put all things under his power" (v. 3, NIV), so in sovereignty he related humility to love, obedience, and foot washing (vv. 1, 34). He began to wash his disciples' feet, a subservient task normally performed by a servant or perhaps by the disciples of an esteemed rabbi. At any rate, like the other tests that we have considered, it was an attention-getting reversal of the customary roles, as evidenced by Jesus' dialogue with Peter in verses 6–10. It was a deliberate lesson on humility to demonstrate the selfless service that would be necessary in the way of suffering and blessing.

The Upper Room Discourse (John 13–17) develops a chain of relationships underlying a full-orbed concept of humility. The relationship of the Father and the Son (13:1–3; 14:9–14) and the Trinitarian relationship with believers (14:15–21; 16:12–16) provide for God's ongoing mission in this hostile world (15:18–16:11). The indwelling Spirit gave peace to the disciples as they began to realize the reality of Jesus' warnings (14:1, 27).[36] The Upper Room is where their naiveté transitioned to anxiety with the realization that the cross was a necessary prelude to kingly glory. In other words, Jesus was not at the wrong place at the wrong time; he was at the right place at the right time. "You do not realize [οἶδα] now what I am doing, but later you will understand [διδάσκω]" (13:7, NIV).[37] What must be understood about humility is that it is inextricably bound to a God-honoring lifestyle rather than a self-based pride where the vices cluster around the use of other

36. Lanier Burns, "John 14:1–27: The Comfort of God's Presence," *Bibliotheca Sacra* 172 (July–September 2015): 299–315.

37. The two terms for "knowing" may be "more or less synonymous" (*TDNT*, s.v. "οἶδα," by Heinrich Seesemann, 5:118), but Jesus suggested a distinction between knowledge as fact and knowledge as comprehension and motivation to obey. In John, knowledge "comes to expression in acts" ("Do you understand what I have *done*?"), a depth of comprehension that produces obedience (cf. *TDNT*, s.v. "γινώσκω," by Rudolf Bultmann, 1:712; *TDNT*, s.v. "οἶδα," by Heinrich Seesemann, 5:118). In other words, one may know about the pride and humility without realizing the consequences of pride or the blessings of humility.

people for personal gain. A tangential concept of humility is sacrificial love (13:3, 34; 14:20–22; 15:9–17), which is a matter of obedience to the Master in mutual service, even to the point of the "greater love," which is martyrdom (15:13). This notion of agapeic love as obedience to Jesus' example and command is crystallized in the lowliness of foot washing. Looking back, we see its continuity with the misunderstanding of the disciples, the willingness to serve without status, and the association of service with suffering.

Peter evidenced their continuing misunderstanding when he balked at Jesus washing their feet: "You shall never wash my feet" (John 13:8). When Jesus declared that without the cleansing, people would have no part with him, Peter changed and requested a bath. "The one who has bathed . . . is completely clean," and the disciples were clean, except for Judas Iscariot (vv. 2, 10–11, 18). Jesus had moved the image of the suffering Savior from a ransom payment to a bath. His sacrifice on the cross cleansed believers from the pollution of sin and made humility a subsequent expectation of salvation.

When he finished washing their feet, Jesus returned to his rabbinical instruction, "Do you understand [γινώσκετε] what I have done? . . . You call me Teacher and Lord [κύριος], and you are right, for so I am" (John 13:12–13). His identity in this setting is an exemplary Master (the meaning of *Lord* here), whose service must be followed. "Now that I, your Lord and Teacher, have washed your feet, you also should wash one another's feet. I have set you an example that you should do as I have done for you."[38]

---

38. In Paul's terms, "Through love serve one another. . . . Bear one another's burdens, and so fulfill the law of Christ" (Gal. 5:13; 6:2). "Washing one another's feet should be taken as an emblem of lowering oneself to meet another's need *whatever* that need happens to be at a particular moment." Andreas Köstenberger, *Encountering John: The Gospel in Historical, Literary, and Theological Perspectives* (Grand Rapids: Baker Academic, 1999), 1947. Similarly, Jonathan Wilson notes, "In his foot washing, Jesus is servant. That is our model. Following Jesus cannot be reduced to a willingness to

The mandate to follow Christ's example accords with a relational principle that other Gospel authors cite as well: "Truly, truly, I say to you, a servant is not greater than his master, nor is a messenger [the only use of ἀπόστολος in John] greater than the one who sent him" (John 13:16; cf. Matt. 10:24–25; Luke 6:40; 22:27). The way of humility is the defining characteristic of the Lord that his disciples must follow. Following his example is the most basic meaning of being a Christian follower. As Ernest Best stated, "'Follow me' is the challenge to those who would be his disciples (Mark 1:17; 1:20; 2:14)."[39] In other words, the servant and messenger share the role and can anticipate the greatness of God who commissioned them. On this basis the lowly and the last are privileges rather than burdens.

Finally, Jesus promises a blessing for humility. "Now that you know [οἴδατε] these things, you will be blessed if you do them" (John 13:17, NIV).[40] We have noted that humility may bring honor rather than shame at a banquet table. This beatitude probably refers to the joy that God gives his humble servants (cf. 17:13). The blessing will sound like foolishness to someone who strives for joy "the old-fashioned way," striving for an earned reward. This joy is a mutual joy that is shared by God and his obedient servants, a gracious gift for our practice of his presence in our lives. Foot washing should be joyful rather than obligatory. It is the joy of friendship (15:15), for "I have told

die for another if the occasion should arise, while ignoring opportunities for service now. . . . Here the example of Christ is not just a willingness to die but a daily laying down of one's life."

39. Ernest Best, *Disciples and Discipleship: Studies in the Gospel According to Mark* (Edinburgh: T&T Clark, 1986), 5. On page 13, Best elaborates on his understanding of discipleship: "What does it mean to follow Jesus? The answer is: It means to drop in behind him, to be ready to go to the cross as he did, to write oneself off in terms of any kind of importance, privilege or right, and to spend one's time only in the service of the needs of others."

40. At a most practical level, the reader should consult John Mitchell Jr., "The Privilege of Being a Servant," in *The Christian in Business* (Westwood, NJ: Fleming Revell, 1962).

you this so that my joy may be in you and that your joy may be complete" (v. 11).

Perhaps a difficulty in understanding biblical joy can be clarified by its outward evidence of "modern laughter." This is laughter that comes from a God-given freedom to see ourselves honestly as creatures of God in a vast universe. It is a release from the burden of feeling that the weight of this sinful world rests on our shoulders and that its insoluble problems continue because our words and deeds are not perfect enough. Since believers are sinners we are released from laughing at the folly of others, which usually reflects our own shortcomings. We are released from the need to express our negative emotions like anger, jealousy, hatred, or various lusts, which reflect our lack of restraint rather than our strengths. And we are released from the indulgence of hedonistic pursuits of our limitless desires. These are forms of pride! Instead we can laugh at ourselves as we encounter the incongruities of our lives. According to David Augsburger, "Humorous humility sees the foolishness of putting on airs, so it smiles at its own pretenses, it recognizes the pettiness of comparing ourselves to one another, so its tongue is always thrust into the cheek of pride: it knows its own selfish bias, so it persistently pokes fun at its own claims to virtue."[41] What Jesus promised is joy when we conquer pride that refuses to wash fellow believers' feet.

Conclusion

The concern for greatness has been a preoccupation of all people. Perhaps for this reason it occupies such a large place in the teaching and practices of Christ's first advent. Two emphases of the great reversal in Christ's ethics are rather shocking to

41. David Augsburger, *Dissident Discipleship: A Spirituality of Self-Surrender, Love of God, and Love of Neighbor* (Grand Rapids: Brazos, 2006). 103.

those of us who have little inclination to deviate from the ways of the world and who stand to lose ill-gotten gain from the less privileged of the world. We have been exploring contrasting perspectives on leadership between oppressive rulers on earth and servant-kings of a very different kingdom. First, there is a pervasive "fame game" in which people will do anything (humane or otherwise) to win and engender personal popularity at the expense of constituencies that they supposedly care about. The biblical way of wisdom calls for a reversal of the values of the world around us, which has canonized pride as a secular virtue and demoted humility to a vice that weakens the strong. Jesus calls believers to a willingness to be socially powerless, which in turn implies a willingness to serve in the lowest role among the least privileged of people, knowing that God will exalt such people in his time and way. For this reason among others, Lewis is irrefutably correct, "Pride leads to every other vice: it is the complete anti-God state of mind. . . . pride always means enmity—it is enmity. And not only enmity between man and man, but enmity to God."[42] Jesus' teaching was designed to foster unity and community among his people. His way of humility is noncomparative and—consequently—noncompetitive, because all sovereignty and power reside in the Creator and Redeemer of the world. Those who practice a humble (i.e., God-centered) lifestyle allow the indwelling Holy Spirit to live through them, like the biblical authors embracing the title of God's slave as a badge of honor.

Second, we have seen that pride and humility are broad concepts occurring in matrices of truth. The attempt to formulate a precise, simple definition of humility will inevitably clash with a plethora of contradictory proposals. Normally humility is viewed as a meek quality that shrinks from a robust approach to life. It

42. Lewis, *Mere Christianity*, 122, 124.

149

is not! Jesus taught about pride and humility as he marched to the cross—surely the most heroic march in history. And when he taught humility, he related it to childlike submission to God—analogous to his own relationship with his Father—and his mission in the world. Such submission mandates a willingness to be lowly and to serve without reservation. It is foot washing: knowing that we should follow our Master even if we have not fully understood his ways. Gordon Keddie correctly emphasized, "There, then, is Jesus' practical benchmark for Christian discipleship: 'You should do as I have done to you.'"[43] In the crucible of love and obedience to the Spirit, our practices are transformed into indicators of our allegiance to Christ and his people. To what extent do we see this kind of commitment in ourselves—and in the church today?

Summary

The Synoptic Gospels move wisdom's counterintuitive ethical reversal to the center of Jesus' incarnational example. His filial devotion to the Father exemplified the way of wisdom for his disciples. The challenges of childlike lowliness, serving people who cannot advance our social status, and trusting God for our significance require substantial maturation over time. Loving God with all of our hearts is the key to biblical greatness. This accords with following our crucified Savior and eagerly anticipating resurrection as he did. It will be manifested in having humble attitudes toward serving God in this hostile world.

---

43. Gordon Keddie, *A Study Commentary on John*, 2 vols. (Auburn, MA: Evangelical Press, 2001), 2:18. Long ago Ezra Gould noted, "But these things, humility and service, in the kingdom of God, not only lead to greatness, they are greatness, i.e., they are the supreme marks of the Christian quality," *A Critical and Exegetical Commentary on the Gospel according to Mark*, ICC (Edinburgh: T&T Clark, 1896), 174.

Key Terms

childlike. Powerless.

discipleship. A synonym for mentoring or investing in the training of believers.

heart. In the Bible, the center or identity of a person.

lowly, last. A willingness to be insignificant in the world as opposed to "royalty."

oppressors. Proud people who take advantage of others for personal gain.

poor. "Poor [humble] in spirit" rather than poverty in property.

principle. A basic truth or foundational standard in a system of beliefs.

promise. In the case of God, an assurance that will come to pass.

ransom. Redemptive payment to release believers from imprisonment to sin.

reflexive. An action with self as both subject and object.

servant-leadership. An eagerness to serve, "not lording it over those entrusted to you" (1 Peter 5:3, NIV).

Questions for Discussion

1. How does Jesus' definition of greatness in his kingdom differ radically from the world's notions of prestige and power?
2. What did Jesus mean when he said, "Unless you turn and become like children, you will never enter the kingdom of heaven" (Matt. 18:3)?
3. What did Jesus mean when he referred to "the kingdom of heaven"?
4. How many people do you know who qualify as great in the eyes of the Savior?
5. How does the Wisdom Literature in the Bible help us to understand Jesus' description of greatness?

see oneself as an object of judgment

6. What did Jesus mean when he said, "Whoever does not take his cross and follow me is not worthy of me" (Matt. 10:38)?

7. How does "losing one's life" lead to finding life in Christ?

8. Why is humility a necessary concept for achieving social and ecclesial unity?

9. Why did John counsel separation from people like Diotrophes? Why did Diotrophes have nothing to do with other believers (cf. 1 John 2:19)?

10. What is Jesus' reasoning in the Gospels behind his pivotally important reversal of values?

11. Why must we remember that biblical humility is not a vow of poverty, an automatic reversal of rank, or the superiority of seniority?

12. What did Jesus mean when he said, "God knows your hearts. For what is exalted among men is an abomination in the sight of God" (Luke 16:15)?

13. Can people become humble apart from God?

14. How does humility describe the ideal of Christlikeness?

15. Was C. S. Lewis correct when he wrote that "pride is essentially competitive"?

16. Do you think that in a day of overwhelming secularity we may have lost any kind of meaningful fellowship with God?

17. How does foot washing exemplify humility and the authority of the Lord (cf. John 13)?

For Further Reading

Burns, Lanier. *The Nearness of God: His Presence with His People.* Phillipsburg, NJ: P&R Publishing, 2009. This book centers on "Incarnation as Presence," which means that Jesus' teaching on pride and humility is God's assessment of the subject.

Yancey, Philip. *The Jesus I Never Knew.* Grand Rapids: Zondervan, 1995. One of the most honest accounts of Jesus in print, which doesn't bypass hard information like "the last will be first." "It would be easier, I sometimes think, if God had given us a set of ideas to mull over and kick around and decide whether to accept or reject. He did not. He gave us himself in the form of a person" (261). Yancey then alludes to C. S. Lewis's famous challenge that Jesus is either a lunatic, or the devil, or the Son of God (263).

6

Christlike Humility
in Paul's Epistles

FACTIONS AND DIVISIONS shatter people, homes, churches, tribal groups, nations, and the world. If they are not addressed properly, they lead to some kind of war. The Bible teaches that the wisdom of the world is earthy, divisive, and flows from selfish ambition, which is pride. Ἐριθεία translates as "selfish ambition" or "factiousness" and leads to "disorder and every evil practice" (James 3:13–16; 4:1–8, NIV). James's audience lusted after pleasures and were mired in fights and quarrels. Pride caused Nebuchadnezzar to become an insane monster until in wisdom he "praised the Most High" (Dan. 4:28–35, NIV). Paul pointed the imperial rulers in the Old Testament toward their eschatological culmination in 2 Thessalonians 2:3–4: "Let no one deceive you in any way. For that day [the return of Christ] will not come, unless the rebellion comes first, and the man of lawlessness is revealed, the son of destruction, who opposes and exalts himself against every so-called god or object of worship, so that he takes his seat in the temple of God, proclaiming himself to be God." Proverbs traced dissension to hatred, greed, envy, and perversity, which are expressions of pride (Prov. 10:12; 15:18; 16:28; 28:25; 29:22). Pride is so insidious that it can divide a church by claiming to follow Christ in a superior way, a kind of ego-trip that gives "nobodies" a sense of superiority over fellow believers. According to Moisés Silva, "The true obstacle to unity is not the presence of legitimate differences of opinion but self-centeredness. Shifting attention away from ourselves becomes the challenge."[1] These self-centered drives fracture marriages, destroy teams, and cause wars between nations.

On the other hand, humility (πρᾶϋτης [James 3:13], ταπεινός [4:6]) leads to godly, biblical wisdom that unifies our personalities, churches, homes, schools, teams and other gatherings of like-minded people. In a cumulative way, the New Testament Epistles build on the prior chapters and complete the antithesis between pride and humility under the following headings:

- Pride as the cause of Philippian disunity
- Humility as the example of Christ
- Humility as the way of biblical greatness
- Pride as the cause of Corinthian disunity
- Humility as Paul's response to Corinthian boasting

The connections between the Epistles and the Gospels are clear. First, the New Testament emphasizes service regardless of status, which is expounded at length in 1 Corinthians 12:12–31. "That there may be no division in the body, but that the members may have the same care for one another" (v. 25). "For as in one body we have many members, and the members do not all have the same function, so we, though many, are one body in Christ, and

1. Moisés Silva, *Philippians*, BECNT, ed. Robert Yarbrough and Robert Stein (Grand Rapids: Baker Academic, 1992), 101.

individually members of one another" (Rom. 12:4–5). "As each has received a gift, use it to serve one another, as good stewards of God's varied grace" (1 Peter 4:10). Second, service is definitive for Christian identity because of the example of the Chief Shepherd, who lived in submission to his Father (1 Peter 2:13–3:6). Peter's exhortation for believers to be "clothed in humility toward one another" (5:5) is widely regarded as an allusion to John 13. Resistant at first, Peter came to understand the importance of foot washing (v. 7).[2] Believers were to "Humble yourselves, therefore, under the mighty hand of God so that at the proper time he may exalt you . . . because he cares for you" (1 Peter 5:6–7). Finally, the connection of humility and community is found in the metaphors of the church, the whole and the parts being woven into a fabric of God's continuing presence on the earth. We are reminded of Ulrich Luz's comments about the "community discourse":

> When the church is not community, it is not the church. For Matthew the key to a life capable of community is *lowliness* (vv. 3–4). Such lowliness requires a change of one's orientation: the renunciation of power, rank, wealth, and self-promotion: the recognition of one's own fallibility and lack of security; taking seriously the other members of the family and always reaching out to them, and direct communication.[3]

Philippians 2 unites the connection of humility with service, Christlikeness, and community in a compact summary of our topic.

---

2. Gerald Hawthorne viewed John 13:3–17 as an almost perfect model for the movement of the Christ hymn (Phil. 2:6–8). Hawthorne and Ralph Martin, *Philippians*, WBC 43 (Nashville: Thomas Nelson, 2004), 103.

3. Ulrich Luz, *Matthew 21–28: A Commentary*, trans. James Crouch, Hermeneia (Minneapolis: Augsburg Fortress, 2005), 478.

Pride as the Cause of Philippian Disunity

Philippians is one of Paul's four prison epistles. It was probably written in the early 60s from Rome. Philip of Macedon, Alexander the Great's father, built the city in 358–57 B.C. on an ancient Thracian site. Over time it was destroyed by wars. Emperor Octavian later rebuilt it as a military outpost, populated it with veterans of his wars, made it a Roman *colonia* and gave it the status of *ius italicum*, the highest honor accorded to Roman cities. Consequently, as citizens of Rome, the Philippians could buy and sell property, were exempt from land and poll taxes, and were entitled to protection under Roman law. Its people were "proud of their city, proud of their ties with Rome, proud to observe Roman customs and obey Roman laws, proud to be Roman citizens."[4] They had a strong desire for public esteem, status markers, and social prestige, which would have carried over to the church.[5] Paul's awareness of Roman opposition to Christian values (Phil. 1:28–30) and internal division in the church (cf. 4:2) prompted the letter. His stated purposes in writing were his thankfulness for their partnership in finances and prayer (1:19; 4:18) and his commendations of his messenger Epaphroditus (2:25) and Timothy, his only emissary "who will be genuinely concerned for your welfare. For they all seek their own interests, not those of Jesus Christ" (2:20–21). We should not be surprised by his exhortation to "let your manner of life be worthy of the gospel of Christ" (1:27; cf. Col. 1:10; Eph. 4:1). Undertones of persecution from Rome and potential fragmentation of the church lie beneath the surface of this otherwise joyful epistle.

4. Gerald Hawthorne, s.v. "Letter to the Philippians," *Dictionary of Paul and His Letters*, ed. G. Hawthorne, R. Martin, and D. Reid (Downers Grove, IL: InterVarsity Press, 1993), 207.

5. Joseph Hellerman, *Reconstructing Honor in Roman Philippi: Carmen Christi as Cursus Pudorum*, SNTSMS, vol. 132, 34.

The portion of Philippians most applicable for our topic is 2:1–11. It begins with the importance of humility for unity (vv. 1–5); it exhorts believers to follow the example of Christ (vv. 6–8); and it illustrates biblical significance according to the pattern of Christ (vv. 9–11). First, as a prelude to 2:1–4, Paul wanted assurance that his readers "are standing firm in one spirit, with one mind striving side by side for the faith of the gospel" (1:27). Without humility, unity would be impossible, and the gospel could not be defended against hostile forces. The church was polarized between factious women, and Paul pleaded with them and the church for a change of attitude (4:2; 2:2).

The foundations of humility are four common benefits of all believers: union with Christ, the comfort of his sacrificial love, the fellowship of the indwelling Spirit, and the clear expectation of Christian compassion. Paul underscores these shared blessings, which are often assumed more than they are practiced. The challenge of the Christian faith is to unite beliefs, which do not change, and ethics, which are usually contingent on social context and circumstances for specific applications. These commonalities normatively prohibited a dangerous self-centeredness that had crept into the church. Paul's joy was contingent on their like-mindedness in love, spirit, and purpose (v. 2). Christians were expected to think and behave in a Christlike way throughout the church's history.

Philippians 2:3 lacks a main verb, so Paul continues to define correct thinking (φρονῆτε, φρονοῦντες) from verse 2: with one mind "do nothing from rivalry or conceit, but in humility count others more significant than yourselves."[6] His point is clear: "Don't think any thoughts that are vainglorious." The verse contains two phrases with the same preposition (κατά, "in conformity with"), which present the mindset that threatened the

---

6. Paul perhaps implies an imperative ποιεῖτε ("do nothing").

church. The first is "rivalry" (or "selfish ambition," cf. James 3:14). Ἐριθεία is rare outside of Scripture and means self-striving for advantage over one's peers. Its motive is to gain wealth and prestige rather than to exemplify service.[7] Gordon Fee noted, "Self-ambition stands at the heart of human fallenness, where self-aggrandizement at the expense of others primarily dictates value and behavior."[8] Consistently in the New Testament the term refers to an obsessive self-seeking that is unable to comprehend higher values.[9]

Κενοδοξία ("vainglory") is from two words meaning "empty" and "honor, glory." Thus, it refers to a futile ambition for self-glorification (or conceited self-ambition).[10] It is a delusion of one's own worth and potential with no thought of God. Taken together, ἐριθεία and κενοδοξία in Philippians 2:3 expose an attitude of competitive self-promotion, which Paul emphatically forbade in his churches.

Instead, believers were to live with "humility of mind" (ταπεινοφροσύνη). The compound was viewed as derogatory in the Hellenistic culture, connoting a shameful, servile attitude. In the Bible it is honored as the essential trait characterizing right relationships with God and others. The Old Testament frequently uses it to describe the Lord exalting the lowly and abasing the proud. In the words of Walter Grundmann,

7. Ceslas Spicq, *Theological Lexicon of the New Testament*, 3 vols., ed. James Ernest (Peabody, MA: Hendrickson, 1994), 2:660.

8. Gordon Fee, *Philippians*, Intervarsity New Testament Commentary Series, ed. Grant Osborne (Downers Grove, IL: InterVarsity Press, 1999), 186.

9. *TDNT*, s.v., "ἐριθεία," by Friedrich Büchsel, 2:661.

10. "The Christian tradition distinguishes pride from vainglory, but also explores the close motivational links between the two. Put briefly, the prideful desire superiority, and the vainglorious desire the *show* of superiority, although these can easily be entangled in practice. (That fact partly explains, I think, why the two vices were merged into one on later lists of the deadly sins.)" Rebecca Konyndyk DeYoung, *Vainglory: The Forgotten Vice* (Grand Rapids: Eerdmans, 2014), 7–8. DeYoung's observation is rather modern in its fine distinctions. Perhaps Paul would not have quibbled in this way with the Philippians.

The term ταπεινοφροσύνη thus catches up what Jesus said about greatness through service. . . . It is given its distinctive shape by Jesus' own conduct, which in Phil. 2:5–11 is viewed from a standpoint which serves as the basis of Paul's admonition, 2:1–4. . . . This has nothing whatever to do with self-disparagement or servility. . . . Only by ταπεινοφροσύνη, refraining from self-assertion, can the unity of the congregation be maintained.[11]

Fee explained unity accordingly, "Here Paul's roots are in the OT—and in Christ. In the OT the term indicated 'lowliness' . . . and the truly humble show themselves so by resting their case with God rather than trusting their own strength and machinations."[12]

Humility of mind, according to Paul, is not passive or timid. It is an aggressive concern for the interests of others (Phil. 2:3–4). He uses ἡγούμενοι in the sense of "consider" or "regard" (also in verse 6 of Jesus' self-humiliation). "Let each person esteem other believers as better than themselves." A believer must look after his own interests responsibly but (ἀλλὰ καὶ) must also serve other believers as needed. Here Paul aligns his counsel with the humility/service mandate of the Gospels. In summary, unity in the church results from having the same Lord and Spirit, avoiding self-aggrandizement, and serving in the interests of fellow believers. Fee refers to this principle as "a vivid, miniature expression of the heart of Pauline ethics."[13]

We would do well to pause and ask why humility is so essential for unity in the church. Paul made no appeal to the virtuousness of the Philippians nor did he appeal to their abilities to overcome the division. His exhortations were based on their

11. *TDNT*, s.v. "ταπεινός," 8:22.
12. Fee, *Philippians*, 188.
13. Ibid., 191.

Trinitarian blessings from God, which should be evidenced in humiliation of self to the extent that they cease from comparison and its concomitant competition for significance. The church should be countercultural to the city. Though he doesn't explicitly make the point, he clearly implied that humility is a mutual God-centeredness and that pride is self-centeredness. If we hark back to the language of the Gospels, believers are to be willing to be last for God's glory. If this is practiced, then there is little room for concern about one's prestige. All glory belongs to God unequivocally, and the ministry of the church is multiplied to the amazement of the world around them (John 17:21). The believers were to sacrificially give for the well-being of the church, so that God could bless them with his significance. They were not to seek to be served but rather to serve and to give themselves to the ministry of the gospel of salvation. Each believer was to use God-given gifts and abilities for the common good of the church without thought as to whose contribution was the greatest. In this perspective, humility is activity for God and his people to the extent that one doesn't even ask if they are being humble. It is a lowly willingness to serve according to the example of Christ.

Humility as the Example of Christ

Philippians 2:5 bridges the exhortation in verses 1–4 with the *carmen Christi* (the "Christ hymn") in verses 6–11, an incarnational summary from the apostolic church.[14] The leading of

14. Ralph Martin, *Carmen Christi: Philippians 2:5–11 in Recent Interpretation and in the Setting of Early Christian Worship*, SNTSMS, vol. 4. According to Martin, the hymn "expressed the quintessential Pauline thought on the person of Christ" (ibid., 21). The passage has been the subject of considerable debate since the work of Ernst Lohmeyer, who shifted the interpretation of the hymn from the biblical context to its background. Lohmeyer viewed the hymn as a cosmic, soteriological drama in heterodox Jewish speculation regarding primal man. *Kyrios Jesus: Eine Untersuchung zu Phil. 2:5–11* (Heidelburg: Heidelburger Akademie der Wiesensch, 1928). Ernst Käsemann and Rudolf Bultmann interpreted the hymn against a Gnostic background (cf. Bultmann's *Theology of the New*

God in all believers is to engender the attitude of Christ in the life of the church: "Your attitude should be the same as that of Christ Jesus."[15] The verse may be paraphrased, "have the same thoughts among yourselves as you should have in your communion with Christ." A correlation of "in Christ Jesus" with "in you" is critical to understanding the relation between the exhortation and the hymn, because the emphasis is on the church's unity of thought and will. Thus, "in you" may be translated "among you" or "toward one another."

Also vital for the meaning of the passage is the conjunction καί ("also") in Philippians 2:5. "In Christ Jesus" in Paul's positional sense makes the καί useless. In the words of Takeshi Nagata, "Only if the exemplary significance of the way of Christ is to be accepted in the sense of conformity of Christians to the way of their savior and lord, Christ, does the use of καί become meaningful."[16] Martin objected, "Paul makes little use of the *imitatio Christi* pattern as a ground for his ethical appeal; and that when he does make an allusion to the example of Jesus it is his earthly life rather than the theological or Christological significance that is drawn upon."[17] Martin's objection falters

---

Testament, 2 vols., trans. Kendrick Grobel [New York: Charles Scribner's Sons, 1951]). Numerous other views and analyses of the passage can be found in Martin, *Carmen Christi*, Appendix B, 313–19. "In summing up these approaches Dr. Martin makes plain his own view that the hymn is not a piece of dogmatic theology, it contains neither an ethical example nor a piece of Christology but 'a piece of Heilsgeschichte.'" Howard Marshall, "The Christ-Hymn in Philippians 2:5–11," *Tyndale Bulletin* 19 (1968), 108. In spite of scholarly detours, the biblical context points to the "ethical example" emphasis, addressing the "pride of mind" that led to division and quarreling in the church. And the separation of the ethical interpretation and a purely soteriological one is misleading in view of Christ's supreme humility on the cross.

15. The verb φρονέω (Phil. 2:5) links verses 1–4 with verses 5–11. The φρον- root appears three times in verses 2–3. Furthermore, ταπεινοφροσύνη (v. 3) corresponds to ἐταπείνωσεν (v. 8); ἡγούμενοι (v. 3) corresponds to ἡγήσατο (v. 6); and κενοδοξίαν (v. 3) corresponds antithetically to ἐκένωσεν (v. 7).

16. Takeshi Nagata, "Philippians 2:5–11: A Case Study in the Contextual Shaping of Early Christology" (PhD diss., Princeton Theological Seminary, 1981), 346.

17. Martin, *Carmen Christi*, 72.

when we note that Paul emphasizes Jesus' incarnate humility, bracketed by his preexistence and exaltation. And Paul used the conformity pattern between Christ and believers elsewhere in his letters (Rom. 15:2–3, 7; Eph. 5:2, 29; Col. 3:13). In summary, Paul is exhorting Christian behavior in keeping with Jesus' example.

What did Christ exemplify in the hymn? Obviously he is unique, and believers cannot live his extraordinarily perfect life or follow his atoning death. His example included his incarnation in the form of a slave, his obedience to death on the cross, and his exaltation to universal worship as Lord to the glory of the Father. We have been called to a willingness to adopt a lowly status in serving others and a willingness to die for God and our fellow believers if necessary. We will receive exaltation from God commensurate with our faithfulness in this life. We are not ἐν μορφῇ θεοῦ, but we should be μορφὴν δούλου ("ministry as servants"). To the world Christian humility is folly, but to believers it is the law of significance in the Trinity's eternal plan. He preexisted as God (ἐν μορφῇ θεου), but he did not selfishly exploit his deity. Instead he "emptied" (ἐκένωσεν) the prerogatives of divine status to assume the form of a slave. He did not empty himself of any aspect of deity; otherwise, he would no longer be God and Savior. The early councils from Nicaea to Chalcedon finalized the hypostatic union of Jesus' two natures in his single person without loss or separation of either nature. With this foundation the hymn shows that humility is a communicable attribute of God, which he ordained for his people as well. As Paul stated in 2 Corinthians 8:9, "For you know the grace of our Lord Jesus Christ, that though he was rich, yet for your sake he became poor, so that you by his poverty might become rich." Instead of personal gain, he considered others better than himself and accomplished their salvation with his substitutionary death.

Μορφή, used twice, refers to "correspondence of form to reality" both of the preexistent Son of the Father (Phil. 2:6) and of servility (v. 7): a stunning combination of a real God and a real servant in a single person. Johannes Behm captures the movement of the passage well: "The appearance assumed by the incarnate Lord, the image of humiliation and obedient submission, stands in sharpest contrast to his former appearance, the image of sovereign divine majesty, whose restoration in a new and even more glorious form is depicted for the exalted κύριος at the conclusion of the hymn, v. 10f."[18] In other words, Paul is reaffirming Christ's instruction in Mark 10:44–45 and parallels; true greatness is sacrificial service, and "the first must be willing to be slave of all," even to the point of laying down our lives for our friends (John 15:13).

As God, the Son condescended through incarnation to the likeness of sinful humanity (cf. John 1:14). Paul's emphasis is on Christ's reflexive initiative (ἑαυτὸν, "he humbled himself"), with the implication that we should empty our vainglorious motives as we pursue obedience in accord with his example of humility. The likeness (ὁμοιώματι) of humanity in this passage means that Christ became fully human but without sin, a concept that is strange to us because all we know is sinful humanity since the fall. We forget that sin is abnormal; it is inherent in fallen human nature. The exaltation of salvation is freedom from the slavery of sin, a return to the service of the Creator. His self-humbling obedience extended to the point of death. His death, which is used twice for emphasis, was crucifixion—the most ignominious, torturous degradation in the Roman era. To Jews it was a curse (Deut. 21:22–23); to Gentiles in general it was punishment for the worst criminals; to Romans, in particular, it was utterly humiliating and offensive. But for God crucifixion is atonement for the

---

18. *TDNT*, s.v. "μορφή," by Johannes Behm, 4:751.

sins of the world, the reconciliation of wrath, love, and justice for the salvation of his people. It was also the way to achieve supreme biblical honor, the gift of a name above all names.[19]

Humility as the Way of Biblical Greatness

Hellerman uses the biblical principle of significance to explain the incentive for the Philippians to follow Jesus' example: "Paul, however, assures his readers of a further reality which, he trusts, will compel those who hear his story fully to embrace his Jesus and to summarily reject prevailing cultural norms: God has assigned to Jesus the highest in honors specifically because of the manner in which Jesus chose to use the power at his disposal."[20] These verses emphatically highlight the reward, response, and purpose of a humble life as exemplified by our Lord Jesus Christ. The exaltation of Jesus is absolutely superlative and unique, but it promises honor for humble believers in God's time and way. This is the explicit promise in the Gospels, which applies implicitly to Paul's readers. Philippians 2:9 refers to a hyper-exaltation commensurate with Jesus' unique humiliation (ὑπερύψωσεν, used only here in the NT). The connection with verses 6–8 is strongly inferential (διὸ καὶ), meaning that Jesus' superlative honor was to be expected on the basis of the biblical principle. God the Father (cf. v. 11) responded to the Son's self-emptying incarnation and crucifixion by graciously giving (ἐχαρίσατο) him the unique name above every name.[21] *Name* in the Bible is

---

19. In a prideful sense, we may note Genesis 11:4: "Come, let us built ourselves a city, with a tower that reaches to the heavens, so that we may make a name for ourselves" (NIV). This clearly illustrates self-centered, ungodly ambition. A godly name is a gift from God, as indicated by his covenants with the patriarchs: "I will make your name great" (Gen. 12:2; 2 Sam. 7:9; of Abraham and David respectively).

20. Hellerman, *Reconstructing Honor*, 148.

21. *Name* occurs 225 times in the NT and only twenty-one times in Paul's epistles. The verb form is found nine times in the NT, and six instances are Paul's.

a description of a person and is equivalent to their identity and character. We have seen that we are to believe and pray in Jesus' name (John 14:13; 16:24; Acts 2:21; 4:12; Eph. 1:21; Heb. 1:4). That is, we call on the One whose character we trust. The name in Philippians 2:9 is incomparable and unique, emphatically above every name, which will ultimately prompt universal worship.

As a result, at the proclamation of Jesus' name every creature and power without exception will bow: angels, earthly populations, and demons. The name might be inexpressible with the limitations of language. In context, it may be "Lord Jesus Christ" and the full theology that it represents (cf. Matt. 28:19; Rom. 1:7; 10:9; 14:9; 1 Cor. 8:6). Philippians 2:10 is an allusion to Isaiah 45:23: "Before me [Yahweh] every knee shall bow, every tongue shall swear allegiance" (NIV). The verse identifies the one and only living God with Jesus and affirms his abiding sovereign deity through his crucifixion and resurrection.

The purpose of exalting the humble Lord and making the last to be first is the glory of God. In worship every human and angelic being will confess that Jesus Christ is Lord to the glory of God the Father. The confession of his full title brings glory to the Father in Trinitarian oneness. If God is all in all, then the foolishness of pride is exposed in all of its vanity. "The Son himself will also be subjected to him who put all things in subjection under him, that God may be all in all" (1 Cor. 15:28). Philippians 2:9–11 affirms absolutely that "man's chief end is to glory God and to enjoy him forever." It also affirms Bill Hull's point that "humility was Jesus' core character trait, the foundation of his influence on others."[22]

In summary, Philippians 2 represents the convergence of aspects of pride and humility that were presented in the Pentateuch, Wisdom Literature, Prophets, and Gospels. The problem

22. Bill Hull, *The Complete Book of Discipleship* (Colorado Springs: NavPress, 2006), 256.

of pride, so vividly illustrated by kings in the Prophets, was now applied to believers in an exemplary church. The results, from factiousness to war, were biblically inevitable. The focus in Philippians 2 is on the example of Christ, who exemplified the aspects of humility that generate unity: an aggressive pursuit of service and an obedience to God's will for the benefit of his people. This was his instruction to his disciples in the Gospels. Because of his extreme sacrifice in crucifixion, the last became first in resurrection. The Father exalted the Son, who chose humility instead of exploiting the powerful privileges of divine status. This is the profound incentive for believers, who "loved the glory that comes from man more than the glory that comes from God" (John 12:43). His "already" will be the "not yet" for his faithful believers. The great reversal is implied in another climactic passage from Paul, "Oh, the depth of the riches of the wisdom and knowledge of God! . . . For from him and through him and to him are all things. To him be the glory forever!" (Rom. 11:33, 36, NIV).

Pride as the Cause of Corinthian Disunity

Any treatment of Paul's view of pride and humility would be incomplete without a consideration of his encounters with pride in Corinth. Philippians is a deeply theological appeal to one of the apostle's favored churches. The Corinthian epistles are Paul's defense of his ministry to a church that had accepted cultural standards instead of basic Christian doctrines. Even more than Philippi, Corinth illustrated the power of context in determining the behavior of populations. Corinth was strategically located on an isthmus between the Ionian and Aegean seas, "the crossroads of Greece."[23] As the hub of the Peloponnesian region, its trade

---

23. Dio Chrysostom, *The Eighth Discourse*, LCL, trans. Lamar Crosby, 5.

flourished and its soil yielded generous harvests.[24] Before the siege of Troy, it existed as Ephure and perhaps received its name from Corinthus, son of Marathon.[25] Its early government was oligarchic under the Bacchiadae, after which power was given to magistrates. Around 550 B.C. its three hundred thousand citizens enjoyed unequaled prosperity. Its arts flourished, especially casting in bronze, making it the ornament of Greece. Jérôme Carcopino eulogized Rome's grandeur by quoting Petronius, "The entire world was in the hands of the victorious Romans. ... Even the simple soldier could caress the bronzes of Corinth."[26] Proverbially proud, the Corinthians insulted the Roman Consul Leucius Mummius, who sacked the city in 146 B.C.[27]

Corinth lay in ruins until Julius Caesar, "the founder of modern Corinth," commissioned a substantial population to rebuild Colonia Iulia Corinthus.[28] It became an imperial province in A.D. 15. It again became a large, prosperous city by the time that Paul arrived for a year and a half of ministry (Acts 18:11).[29] The Isthmian games were surpassed in prestige only by the Olympian games, and the president of the games (the *agonothetes*) was the city's highest ranking official. At the time of the New Testament, Corinth was comparatively new and "wealthy because of its commerce."[30] Its ambitious people were largely *nouveaux riches* merchants and craftsmen. According to Timothy Savage,

24. Macedonius noted that Demeter "never reaped rich Corinthian harvests, but never tasted bitter poverty," in *The Greek Anthology*, trans. W. R. Paton, LCL (Cambridge: Harvard University Press, 1969), 1:319.

25. Pausanius, *Description of Greece*, LCL, 1:1.

26. Jérôme Carcopino, *Daily Life in Ancient Rome: The People and the City at the Height of the Empire*, trans. E. O. Lorimer (New Haven: Yale University Press, 1940), 174.

27. Pausanius, *Description of Greece*, 1:2.

28. Ibid, 3:1; Strabo, *Geography*, trans. Horace Leonard Jones, LCL, 8.6.23; The settlers were largely "freedmen, whose status as manumitted servants were just above slaves. The city also had a significant component of Jews as a hub of the Jewish Diaspora." Dio, *Roman History*, LCL, 21.

29. Appian, *Roman History*, LCL, 8.136.

30. Strabo, *Geography*, 8.6.20.

"It became the envy of the Empire—a city of pleasure, a tribute to human-made splendor, a place where assertiveness and pride reaped great reward."[31]

The ethics of Corinth were tethered to its illustrious past, its fortuitous location, and its imperial prestige. Its citizens placed their premium on status, wealth, and personal power; that is, any behavior that would suggest their superiority over other people. This resulted in extravagant self-display and boasting with concomitant denigration of the powerless and poor.[32] Horace noted, "To achieve great deeds and to display captivating powers to one's fellow-citizens is to touch the throne of Jove and to scale the skies. Yet to have won favour with the foremost men is not the lowest glory. It is not every man's lot to get to Corinth."[33]

The latter sentence, "non cuivis homini contingit adire Corinthum," was a well-known motto of the city's upscale reputation and loose morals. The projection of status was crucial, but honor was given only for visual displays to promote public admiration. Pride was a virtue, and boasting brought celebrity for all to hear. Aristeas requested a statue of himself, so that his fame would never be destroyed. "Fame is never destroyed . . . judgement plays no tricks on any man of worth."[34] The city assessed its citizens by their self-assertiveness and overt braggadocio. The gods reflected the ethos. People yearned for divine power to undergird their standing; the most prosperous citizens evidenced the favor of the most powerful deities to avert misfortune. With no concern for doctrine, their ambitions gravitated to displays of wealth and power. Perhaps Corinth's

31. Timothy B. Savage, *Power through Weakness: Paul's Understanding of the Christian Ministry in 2 Corinthians*, SNTSMS, vol. 86, 52.

32. For example, Aristides dismisses the common people with the following aside: "the greatest things are beyond the masses." *In Defense of Oratory* 46, LCL, trans. C. A. Behr, 307. See also Juvenal, *Satire*, LCL, 3.140–85; Petronius, *Satyricon*, LCL, 57.

33. Horace, *Epistles* 1.17.33–36, LCL, trans. Rushton Fairclough, 363.

34. Chrysostom, *The Thirty-Seventh Discourse*, 47. Also Tacitus, *Annals*, 38.

most important landmark was the Acrocorinthus, a prominent hill that was crowned by a temple of Aphrodite. In Paul's time the shrine was maintained with one thousand prostitutes.[35] The values of the city in the first century have been summarized well by Savage: "In Corinth, perhaps more than anywhere else, social ascent was the goal, boasting and self-display the means, personal power and glory the reward."[36]

In the Corinthian epistles Paul defends his ministry against four criticisms by unnamed opponents: his opposition to boasting, his unimpressive appearance, his inferior speech, and his refusal to accept financial support. Paul was disturbed by the accusations of "false apostles" and by the failure of his converts to support him.[37] His converts had received the proud intruders and turned against Paul for his refusal to follow Corinthian cultural norms. We can infer from textual details that the opponents exemplified the spirit of the city and corrupted Paul's allegiance to Christ as exemplary, humble Savior and the gospel as a gracious accomplishment of the cross. In Fee's words, "Although they were the Christian church in Corinth, an inordinate amount of Corinth was yet in them, emerging in a number of attitudes and behaviors that required radical surgery without killing the patient."[38] His suffering was not a sign of the inferiority of his ministry or of the worthlessness of his message. Paul thanked God for leading him in the way

35. Strabo, *Geography*, 8.6.20.

36. Savage, *Power through Weakness*, 41. Gordon Fee concludes, "All of this evidence together would suggest that Paul's Corinth was at once the New York, Los Angeles, and Las Vegas of the ancient world." *The New International Commentary on the First Epistle to the Corinthians*, rev. ed. (Grand Rapids: Eerdmans, 1987), 3.

37. Savage, *Power through Weakness*, 10. "What has hindered scholars is the paucity of explicit information on the opponents. All we *really* know is that they were Jewish (2 Corinthians 11:22) and outsiders (11:4). Beyond that we may infer that they preached a different Jesus from Paul (11:4), were intruding into his sphere of ministry (10:12–18), were receiving financial support (11:12) and were behaving in a heavy handed manner (11:18–20)."

38. Fee, *First Corinthians*, 4.

of Christ in which the smell of death was transformed into the fragrance of life (2 Cor. 2:14-17), because God's power was evident in his weakness (11:29-30). His ministry of suffering in the Spirit supported his true apostleship. The suffering and the calling were allowed by God to demonstrate the reality of the new covenant (3:7-18). For our purpose, the most germane of the criticisms is his refusal to boast.[39]

The predictable result of pride was quarreling and divisions in the church. "For it has been reported to me by Chloe's people that there is quarreling among you, my brothers" (1 Cor. 1:11). Paul added later: "For I fear that perhaps when I come I may find you not as I wish, and that you may find me not as you wish—that perhaps there may be quarreling, jealousy, anger, hostility, slander, gossip, conceit, and disorder" (2 Cor. 12:20). Paul's word for arrogance (or conceit) is φυσίωσις, which refers to pride as inflation of mind (the opposite of ταπεινοφροσύνη in Phil. 2:3; cf. 1 Cor. 8:1). He uses the term of people who claimed superiority over other Christians. If they were "biblical," then "none of you may be puffed up in favor of one against another. For who sees anything different in you? . . . [W]hy do you boast as if you did not receive it [receive salvation as God's gift]?" (1 Cor. 4:6-7). The

39. The verb καθχάομαι ("to boast") and its cognates are used thirty-nine times in 1 and 2 Corinthians, as opposed to only fifteen times elsewhere in Paul's writings. *Boasting* referred to a cluster of concepts including glorifying and praising, which could apply to God (legitimately) or people (illegitimately) in this context. Fee notes cogently that in the Corinthian epistles, "It comes very close to the concept of 'trust,' that is, 'to put one's confidence in.'" *First Corinthians*, 88. The Corinthians had placed their confidence in the standards of their culture, which is all too common in any age. To the contrary, Paul trusted the example of Christ and the accomplishment of the cross.

Paul's Corinthian correspondence may have included at least four letters. He alludes to a severe letter (2 Cor. 2:3-4), which underscored the strained relations between the true apostle and a group of immoral, insubordinate Christians. Although 1 and 2 Corinthians differ in details of content and tone, for our subject they are thematically unified. Therefore, we will blend the letters on the contrast between pride and humility. The reader can consult D. R. Hall, *The Unity of the Corinthian Correspondence*, Journal for the Study of the New Testament Supplement Series, vol. 251 (London: T&T Clark, 2003).

ground is level at the foot of the cross, and grace means that we can bring nothing (personally or culturally) to gain advantage with God. His opponents are arrogant in their claims of being superior agents of divine power (vv. 18–19). And "love does not envy or boast; it is not arrogant" (13:4). In 2 Corinthians 12:20 arrogance is embedded in self-centered sins that manifested the core problem of pride. Φυσίωσις was the foundational problem in the Corinthian opposition to Paul's ministry, and boasting was the outward reflection of the inner problem.[40]

The behavioral form of pride that Paul was addressing was a claim to follow Paul, Apollos, Cephas, or Christ as more prestigious alternatives to Christian living. This contradicted Paul's instruction in Philippians 2 as well as the gospel according to the cross in the Gospels (1 Cor. 1:17; 2:2–5). The way to be great, they held, was to conform to Corinth's standards. This was a confusing problem that perverted good people into false allegiances to men rather than to God. In the words of Scott Hafemann, "At the heart of the issue is the opponents' claim that they, not Paul, represent and are equal to the 'eminent apostles' in Jerusalem. In this section Paul endeavors to show that he is the one who is a genuine apostle, on a par with the leaders of the mother church (2 Cor. 11:5; 12:11)."[41] At issue was the growth and unity of the church. Therefore, Paul urgently explains: "But I, brothers, could not address you as spiritual people, but as people of the flesh, as infants in Christ. . . . For you are still of the flesh. For while there is jealousy and strife among you, are you not of the flesh and behaving only in a human way? For when one says, 'I follow Paul,' and another, 'I follow Apollos,' are you not being

40. Two of the other terms are familiar to us by now. Ἐριθεία ("selfish ambition") is the term that was used in Philippians of the attitude that led to quarrels and divisions. Ἀκαταστασία ("disorders") here seems to point to "self-seeking."

41. Scott Hafemann, "Letters to the Corinthians," in *Dictionary of Paul and His Letters*, ed. Gerald Hawthorne, Ralph Martin, and Daniel Reid (Downers Grove, IL: InterVarsity Press, 1993), 171.

merely human?" (1 Cor. 3:1, 3–4). The reference to "mere men" seems to highlight pride as the ingrained, characteristic condition of sinful humanity.

Humility as Paul's Response to Corinthian Boasting

Paul answers Corinthian pride with a single principle based on a quote of Jeremiah 9:24: "as it is written, 'Let the one who boasts, boast in the Lord'" (1 Cor. 1:31; cf. 2 Cor. 10:17). Paul argues the superiority of God's wisdom versus the foolishness of the world's thinking. "None of the rulers of this age understood this," he argued, "for if they had, they would not have crucified the Lord of glory" (2:8). In 2 Corinthians he describes unbelief as blindness. "In their case the god of this world has blinded the minds of the unbelievers, to keep them from seeing the light of the gospel of the glory of Christ, who is the image of God" (4:4).[42]

To support the principle, Paul underscored God's calling of himself and the Corinthians (1 Cor. 1:1, 26). Paul was appointed to be an apostle of Christ Jesus, as distinct from his cosigners Sosthenes and Timothy, who were mere brothers in the faith (1 Cor. 1:1; 2 Cor. 1:1). Paul's status as a true apostle had been attacked by his opponents, so this distinction was a critical entry point for his defense. In Corinth "not many of you were wise according to worldly standards, not many were powerful, not many were of noble birth" (1 Cor. 1:26). Paul is not saying that the noble and wealthy cannot be saved, but he does imply that worldly status does make following Christ difficult. However, as Fee notes, "For Paul, the glory of the gospel does not lie there; rather it lies in God's mercy toward the very people whom most of the

---

42. Elsewhere Paul describes satanic enemies as "servants of righteousness" under the "angel of light" (2 Cor. 11:14–15). So deception blurred the line between true and false ministers.

affluent tend to write off—the foolish, the weak, the despised."[43]
In principle "Jews demand signs and Greeks seek wisdom, but we
preach Christ crucified, a stumbling block to Jews and folly to
Gentiles" (v. 23). God, with exclusive authority, chose the foolish
things and the weak and lowly people of the world to shame and
nullify the world's transitory values, so that no one may boast in
his presence (vv. 27–29). Jeremiah 9:23–24 forbids self-boasting
by the wise, the strong, and the rich.[44] This principle emphasizes
that all boasting should be grounded on a relationship with the
Lord, who builds his church up through humble saints.

Paul went beyond Jeremiah to explain why prideful boasting
is useless negatively and positively. Negatively, God exposed the
vanity of boasting by humiliating proud and powerful rulers,
including Nebuchadnezzar. Positively, God exalted the humble
"in Christ Jesus, who has become for us wisdom from God—that
is, our righteousness, holiness, and redemption" (1 Cor. 1:30,
NIV; cf. 2 Cor. 10:1). Since God has provided for all our needs in
Christ—salvation and significance—Christians should boast
only in the Lord.[45] "So then, no more boasting about men!"
(1 Cor. 4:21; 5:6). Paul's ministry was founded on "Jesus Christ
and him crucified," so his defense is his humility in seeking
glory for God and not himself (2:1–5). According to Savage, "It is
precisely his humility which authenticates his status as a minister of the glorious gospel of Christ. . . . On the one hand, few

---

43. Fee, *First Corinthians*, 92.

44. Alfred Plummer and Archibald Robertson note, "The occurrence of 'the wise'
and 'the strong' and 'the rich' (as in v. 26 here) makes the quotation very apt." *A Critical
and Exegetical Commentary on the First Epistle of St. Paul to the Corinthians*, rev. ed., ICC
(Edinburgh: T&T Clark, 1914), 28.

45. Leon Morris notes that the qualities (righteousness, sanctification, and redemption) that characterize godly wisdom are subordinate to it and explain it. The effect
is that all relationship with God is embodied in Christ, so to him be credit and glory.
The First Epistle of Paul to the Corinthians: An Introduction and Commentary (Grand
Rapids: Eerdmans, 1958), 50. Morris's previous comment is apropos: "Christ is the very
atmosphere in which he [Paul] lives." Ibid., 49.

see anything impressive in the ministry of the humble Paul. On the other hand, Paul sees nothing impressive apart from humility."[46] To claim any credit for God's accomplishment is "self-commendation," a measure of self by self. Paul went back to the Pentateuch for the precedent for his charge: "Just as Eve was deceived by the serpent's cunning, [the Corinthians' minds] may somehow be led astray from a sincere and pure devotion to Christ" (2 Cor. 10:12–11:3, NIV). It is "not the one who commends himself who is approved, but the one whom the Lord commends" (10:18). The proper praise of God stands in antithesis to self-praise in Paul's explanation.

Paul felt intense pressure from the culture and the church to boast about himself to defend his founding their church as "a skilled master builder" (1 Cor. 3:10). "Accept me as a fool, so that I too may boast a little. What I am saying with this boastful confidence, I say not with the Lord's authority but as a fool. Since many boast according to the flesh, I too will boast" (2 Cor. 11:16–18). So powerful is conceit that it enslaves, exploits, or bullies other people for personal gain. Paul boasted in two ways. First, he reminded the believers of his qualifications for apostolic leadership. He had a distinguished Jewish heritage, which linked him with the roots of the church in Jerusalem (v. 22). He had suffered for the gospel ministry *par excellence* (vv. 23–29). And he had experienced the inexpressible realities of paradise (12:1–5).[47] At first sight this recital seems to contradict everything that he had argued about the nonsense of self-centered self-aggrandizement. On the other hand, the

---

46. Savage, *Power through Weakness*, 162.

47. It seems strange that Paul would give such detailed information to a church that he founded and loved with pastoral passion. Perhaps he was only reviewing what he had already shared with them. Would we not repeat our legacy, sufferings, and privileged experiences frequently? We might conclude that Paul "boasted in the Lord" to the extent that he did not parade personal information and how, with great hesitation, he gives them his credentials for true apostleship.

calling of God had ordered "spheres of ministries" (or boundaries of influence). Paul was boasting in the Lord because God had assigned the founding and nurture of the Corinthians to him. His opponents were on his God-ordained turf, and they were threatening his reputation and the gospel of Christ. Paul was obligated to vigorously defend what God had accomplished through him, or he would have abdicated his responsibility before the Lord (10:13).

Second, he boasted in the Lord in accord with his governing principle (2 Cor. 10:17).[48] Thus, he limited his boasting to his weaknesses, because this approach demonstrated that his incomparable ministry had resulted from God's working through his humble submission. This was the logical argument that the Lord had made about greatness in the Gospels: trust in God's power rather than personal powers for success in kingdom work. Paul's metaphor was that the light of God in the darkness of the world was to be seen through the earthen vessels of humble believers "to show that the surpassing power belongs to God and not to us" (4:7). In the Graeco-Roman culture the first warrior to scale the wall of the city would be given heroic honors. Paul noted that, instead of heroic ascent, he was lowered from a window to escape because God's power was evident in his weakness (11:30-33). To perpetuate his humility after his "surpassing greatness of the revelations," God allowed Satan to torment him with an unspecified "thorn . . . in the flesh," because "[God's] grace is sufficient for you, for [his] power is made perfect in weakness . . . so that the power of Christ may rest on me. . . . For when I am weak, then I am strong" (12:7-10; cf. 1 Cor. 2:3-5). Paul's logic (cf. 2 Cor. 10:5) is now complete: boasting in the Lord is humility and brings glory to God; in

48. It is instructive to note that when Paul and Barnabas returned from their first missionary journey, they informed the church at Antioch about "all that God had done with them, and how he had opened the door of faith to the Gentiles" (Acts 14:27).

turn the God of glory exalts humble believers and makes them great like Paul.

Paul provided a helpful synthesis on the contrast between pride and humility by reflecting the emphases of the Pentateuch through the Gospels. His teaching about the danger of pride and the need for humility in Philippi and Corinth was complemented by Peter and James; all of the New Testament authors warned about the divisiveness of pride in the churches. The matrix of Christ resurfaces with a focus on sacrificial service with an exemplary humility of mind. Both Philippi and Corinth were proud cities and illustrate the powerful effect that culture exerts on Christian ethics. Pride is presented in Philippians 2 as "selfish ambition" and "vainglory," which threatened the unity of the church. The example of Christ points to the lowliness of crucifixion. According to the biblical principle of God's exaltation of humility, the ascended Messiah was honored with unsurpassable greatness. In the Christ hymn, humility is forcefully communicated as a communicable attribute of God, meaning that it should characterize his people. God does not take away our need for significance, but he transforms needs into blessings as we allow him to live through us. The "name above every name" proved that the last became first in resurrection and ascension. For us this is a primary expectation of our eschatological hope. Corinth illustrated the same warnings and needs even more vividly. The city was a center of pride and pleasures in the empire, and the quarreling church followed the culture in boasting about its members' prestige. Arrogant opponents attacked Paul, the character of Christ, and their cross-shaped humility. Paul responded that all relationships with God, both salvation and calling, were divine gifts and enablement; therefore, "Let him who boasts boast only in the Lord." Humility—not pride—is the proper credential for ministry, because God's power is made evident in our weakness.

Summary

Paul synthesized the biblical emphasis on pride and humility through the lenses of Philippi and Corinth. Other epistles affirmed his warnings—on the one hand the divisiveness of pride, and on the other the necessity of sacrificial service for successful ministry. In Philippians 2 Christ's exaltation with "a name above all names" demonstrated that the church does not need to do the will of God in the ways of the world. Our God-given names are a significant part of our eschatological hope. Humility explicitly is made a communicable attribute of Christ, which should characterize his people as well. In Corinth arrogant opponents attacked Paul for his cross-shaped humility. Paul responded that God has given life and enablement to his people, so that his power can be evident through our weaknesses. For this reason, "we should boast only in the Lord." Pride evidences a severe anemia in one's view of God. His greatness levels our concerns about our comparative importance.

Key Terms

Aphrodite. The Greek goddess of fertility and beauty (the Roman Venus).

braggadocio. Boasting with swagger and pretention.

communicable attribute. A characteristic shared by God and his people, as distinct from an incommunicable attribute such as infinity.

humility of mind. Absence of conceit and selfish ambition; an aggressive concern for the interests of others.

name. In the Bible the identity, character, and reputation of a person.

vainglory. A futile delusion of one's own worth, with little to no thought of God.

Questions for Discussion

1. What are the challenges of a church in a proud culture?
2. Do you agree that Philippians 2:1–4 is a "miniature expression at the heart of Pauline ethics"?
3. If Philippians 2 expresses "the quintessential Pauline thought on the person of Christ," where should we place it in our theological priorities?
4. How does man as the image of God in Genesis 1 inform our understanding of Christ as the express image of God—fully God and fully human in one Person—in the New Testament?
5. In what ways does "touching the throne of Jove and scaling the stars" remind us of Babylon and the propensity of its people in city building?
6. How is pride related to the pursuit of celebrity?
7. How did the Corinthians relate prosperity to their version of misfortune?
8. What happened to Paul when he refused to follow cultural norms that were opposed to humility?
9. What did Paul mean when he said, "I had to address you as people of the flesh"?
10. How should we respond to Paul's observation that "the rulers of this age" are blind, as demonstrated by their crucifixion of Christ?
11. Why has God chosen the weak and lowly people to do his work on earth?
12. How should we view Paul's clear prohibition, "So, then, no more boasting about men!" (1 Cor. 4:21; 5:6)?

For Further Reading

DeYoung, Rebecca Konyndyk. *Vainglory: The Forgotten Vice*. Grand Rapids: Eerdmans, 2014. A highly recommended analysis of "the capital vice of modern culture." Her third chapter, "Vainglory's Roots: Pride and Fear," is especially relevant for this volume.

Savage, Timothy B. *Power through Weakness: Paul's Understanding of the Christian Ministry in 2 Corinthians.* SNTSMS, vol. 86. An outstanding analysis of the city and Paul's defense in language that is applicable to Christian workers.

Whitfield, Charles, et al. *The Power of Humility: Choosing Peace over Conflict in Relationships.* Deerfield, FL: Health Communications, 2006. This is a humanistic approach to conflict resolution that argues that humility is needed to heal the pervasive problem of conflicts. Its approach stands in sharp contrast to Paul's counsel to the Philippians and the Corinthians.

7

Conclusion

Summary of the Study

God created Adam and Eve for covenantal relationship with himself and ordained that we would rule the world. Humanity's dominion is foundational for understanding pride (as self-centeredness) and humility (as God-centeredness), for the two are antithetical responses to God's will for life on earth. From the beginning obedience indicated humble submission to the Word of God. The tempter insidiously played on Adam and Eve's exalted creation in the image of God to suggest that they could rule without creaturely limitation—they could know good and evil, be like God, and not die (Gen. 2:9, 17; 3:4, 22). The presumption that creatures can be Creator is the engine of sin, a rebellion that has short-circuited the Creator's blessings through history.

From this point forward, without a biblical understanding of God, there was no meaningful concept of sin, only the inexplicable evil of man's inhumanity to man. However, this cannot explain the pervasive corruptions and death that fill the pages of history. Sin is basically pride that rebels against creaturely limitations. Fallen image-bearers have been capable of impressive accomplishments, whether good or evil, depending on the orientation of the person toward God. All kinds of people have accomplished intellectual, social, and technological discoveries that have enhanced life on earth, but believers alone have experienced relationship with God with eternal consequences. A meaningful concept of humility can only be traced to an attitude of loving obedience to the Word of God, which undergirds a love of neighbor and self. In other words, humility is the dedication of our ambitions and abilities to God for his glory, trusting him for our security and personal significance.

Humility is implied in Abram's pilgrimage by faith and God's promise of "a great name" for a godly "walk." In line with the Pentateuchal emphasis, Moses' humility was marked by his prayerful pleas to God in contrast to the prideful rebellions of other leaders, his siblings, and the Israelites in general. "The Lord heard his prayers" and blessed this chosen servant. Because Moses was "more humble than anyone else" (Num. 12:3), God revealed himself with personal intimacy. This paradigm is very significant for an understanding of humility and pride in the duration of Scripture. Humility in the Bible is never passive resignation or a sense of self-depreciating worthlessness. It looks diligently for God's will, whatever that may be, but it does not forget that God enables our work and provides the increase. Pride leaves God out of the equation of success, as indicated by failure to obey his commands. "My power and the might of my hand have gotten me this wealth" (Deut. 8:17). God opposes such arrogance without exception!

In matters of life and death we should care deeply that our relationship with God rests on a solid foundation. We should trust in time-tested principles to guide us through the labyrinth of life. Pride as sin and humility as godliness are emphasized from the beginning as the opposing ways of life; pride leads to self-destructive sins, while humility spawns blessed character traits by the grace of God. We are not given detailed definitions or descriptions in the Pentateuch, but we are exposed to narratives that graphically depict the consequences of behavior. Moses, a challenged pilgrim, was "most humble" and enjoyed an extraordinary relationship with God.

I left the Bible's beginnings with a clear sense of the contrast between pride and humility as the opposing ways of life. I have loved pride without knowing it and rejoiced with every personal accomplishment. I used to feel that life was a broad waterway that could only be crossed on the stepping stones of recognition and rewards. If you missed the stones, you would drown in insignificance! I never seemed to realize that this is the way of pride as exemplified by Korah, Dathan, Abiram, Miriam, and Aaron (Num. 12; 16): "You exalt yourselves above the assembly of the LORD" (16:3). The Pentateuchal material is clear that our abilities and efforts are vain without the Lord's enablement. Humility is a time-tested foundation for righteous living.

In the Wisdom Literature, the book of Job discusses at length the popular wisdom that suffering is caused by unconfessed sin. By the same token, the popular view taught that prosperous people are perceived to be blessed because they are righteous. In response to such so-called wisdom, we should humbly confess our inability to fully understand God or life. Without such limitations we should persevere in submission to his will in spite of adverse circumstances. "I do not occupy myself with things too great and too marvelous for me" (Ps. 131:1).

The Psalms and Proverbs divide people into wicked/foolish and righteous/wise categories. The proud, even in Israel, oppressed the poor who sought refuge in the Lord. The wicked became wealthier, which compounded their arrogance and self-sufficiency (Ps. 62:10). Unlike the oppressed psalmists, the prideful persecutors dismissed God as irrelevant in attitude, speech, demeanor, and behavior. Instead they turned to false gods who sanctioned their practices (40:4). Thus, pride was the godless uplifting of self that twisted and perverted justice at the cost of human life and dignity. On the other hand, humble believers were to seek the Lord's intervention on their behalf. Instead of passivity, humility is a confidence that God will judge arrogance (Deut. 32:35; Rom. 12:9). "For you save a humble people," David declared, "but the haughty eyes you bring down" (Ps. 18:27). Believers rested on God's promise that their prayers would be answered and that they would inherit the land of blessing. Saul and David illustrated the stark contrast between pride and humility by showing that humility makes no sense in a narrative without God.

Proverbs brings the humiliation of pride and God's exaltation of the humble to the fore (Prov. 3:34–35; 11:2; 13:10). Humility is a primary indication of wise living. Pride "goes before a fall," because it focuses on short-term self-interests. Godly values promote loving relationships through the presence of God among his people. James 4 and 1 Peter 5 quote Proverbs 3 to reinforce the theme that "a priority for God is the foundation of humility." James attributes humility to the indwelling Spirit, which leads to a depth of understanding that is gained through sacrificial love of God. Peter connected humility under God with community among believers. We must be "clothed" with reciprocal humility as we trust God for his strength in our trials. The humble person will necessarily be teachable (Prov. 13:10). The proud person, on the other hand, is characterized by egotistical thoughts, greed for unjust gain, slanderous speech, and a refusal to listen to biblical wisdom (15:25–33). So deeply entrenched is pride that only the grace of God can penetrate and transform it. The uniquely evil nature of pride opposes the fear of the Lord and the two great commandments of love that flow from it.

One of the hardest things for us to understand is that a humble, godly life may not lead to prosperity and the good life that we hope for. Why do bad things happen to good people like Job? The book of Job addresses this question as one of its main themes. We are nurtured with an expectation that if we try to be good, we will be rewarded with success, prosperity, and happiness. Suffering is universal in a sin-stained world, so humility under God means that sometimes I must acknowledge my inability to understand and explain adversity. I have discovered in major illnesses and surgeries that suffering is beneficial; it causes me to realize my own fragility and need for dependence on the Lord. As I have observed life in light of the Psalms and Proverbs, I can see that wealth often comes at the cost of unethical practices and oppression of the poor. Without a biblical understanding of God, the pursuit of wealth and prestige makes sense, because pride is the socially acceptable way to pursue success in the world. Humble believers should aggressively seek the Lord's intervention, knowing that only his grace can transform pride. Biblical wisdom asks us, "Do we love God that much?" Ultimately we know that God answers prayer and will give the earth to the meek. We should love with a view to long-term "capital gain": godly investments with God's plan and purpose in view. Pride goes before a fall, and a priority for God is the foundation of humility.

The Prophets continued the emphasis on the Lord's exaltation of the humble and humiliation of the proud with vivid imagery. The books contain memorable oracles against proud emperors, with a promise that God would exalt the humble in "his day." The issue again is humility as God-centeredness. The Bible consistently views empires as enemies of God because of their pride—a continuum of overweening ambition to claim the sovereign prerogatives of the almighty Creator in the Pentateuch. Mesopotamia, Egypt, and Tyre join lesser powers with idolatrous claims. God acts in history so that "they will know that I am the Lord." And the undeniable lesson is that pride goes before a fall.

Ezekiel 26–28 is directed against Tyre's influential wealth and seemingly invulnerable position. Wealth is power, and greed promoted an arrogant spirit of invincibility. The pride of the city was exemplified by its king (Ezek. 28). His extraordinary skill in acquiring wealth led him to delusional claims of deity. The oracle looked back to Eden and the cherub who invaded God's paradise and infected the father of proud worldly rulers with an insatiable desire to play God. The consequent insanity of evil has been the scourge of our dying world ever since.

One of Isaiah's most notable oracles was against Babylon (Isa. 14), the archetype of imperial pride. The "oracles against the nations" are the context for the Lord's ultimate worldwide judgment on the pride of unbelief and idolatry: "I will put an end to the pomp of the arrogant, and lay low the pompous pride of the ruthless" (13:11). Proud people are condemned for their disregard of God that led to their oppression of fellow human beings. As in Ezekiel, the reward of pride is death as the great equalizer. As in the Pentateuch, the delusion of divine claims is structured around the opposing height of God-defying arrogance and depth of destiny.

The king of Babylon's pride came to the fore in his resolve, "I will make myself like the Most High." Isaiah's use of the imagery is polemical, looking back to the garden, the expulsion for prideful disobedience, and the scattering of "the great city." The hubristic words express the intention of the Babylonian power or spirit: a Nebuchadnezzar-like representation of Babylonian arrogance. The curse for pride was death, removing any suggestion in the Bible that pride could be perceived as positive. Throughout the Bible we are warned that the rulers' arrogance applies to all sinners and that their ultimate punishment, namely death, is the human condition. Daniel illustrates God's humiliation of pride with Nebuchadnezzar's humiliation—a mighty ruler who changed from persecutor of God's people to a proclaimer of God's dominion over the earth. Again, the purpose was that all people might know that the Most High rules creation. Daniel illustrates dependence upon God's sovereign providence, exemplifying humility and extending grace and mercy to the oppressed.

The lessons of the Pentateuch and Wisdom Literature are portrayed with vivid imagery in the Prophets. Ezekiel traces imperial arrogance to the deception in Eden. Israel struggled to see the sovereignty of God behind imposing and oppressive worldly powers. The struggle is ours as well—centuries later. The Bible consistently tells us that world powers are enemies of God because they try to claim the prerogatives of the almighty Creator. I must continually remind myself that God will win: "I will punish the world for its evil, and the wicked for their iniquity; I will put an end to the pomp of the arrogant, and lay low the pompous pride of the ruthless" (Isa. 13:11). We will cele-brate God's ultimate victory and a universal transformation at the return of the Lord.

The Gospels moved Proverbs' counterintuitive reversal of values to the center of Jesus' ethical agenda. Its promise is that God will humiliate the proud and will exalt the humble believ-ers. The theme of humility as service to the lowly is the tapes-try which frames his teaching. In Matthew 18, Mark 9–10, and Luke 9, greatness depends on a willingness to serve in a lowly way. The impulse of the disciples was to enhance their prestige in the kingdom, which was at odds with the sacrificial standard of their Lord. His life exemplified a willingness to live humbly in service to the humblest of people, which was the defining characteristic of greatness in his kingdom.

This is familial devotion rather than a vague contest for future rewards; as the Son lived in submission to the Father, so believers should mutually serve one another. Humility is sacrificial commitment to the Lord in whatever circumstances we find ourselves instead of the self-centered ambition that characterizes the world. The willingness to be last (the least honorable) is the opposite of Diotrephes (and the Pharisees), "who loved to be first" at the expense of unity and Christian fellowship. Believers should release their worldly pride to allow God to graciously work through them. This does not mean a poverty vow, an automatic reversal of status, or the respectful honor of seniority. The biblical law (or principle) of significance is humble submission to God as a prelude to his exaltation, at the very center of Jesus' mission in the world (Mark 10:43–45).

The Gospels are the hinge of the study—the matrix of its themes is central to the teaching of Messiah. Because of who he is, God incarnate and Savior of mankind, all believers must pay careful attention to his use of biblical wisdom to reverse worldly values. Personally, I have been surprised by my own discomfort with his clear criteria for greatness in his kingdom. The challenges of childlike powerlessness, the call to serve people who cannot advance our social status, and trusting God for our significance in life requires extraordinary maturity. How do we explain such counterintuitive guidance to our families and friends, who embrace the "foolishness" of the world?

Since the world's understanding is blind to godly values, we probably cannot communicate things that are so dependent on the Spirit's transforming presence in believers' lives. But we can remember that the Teacher, though crucified by the world, was resurrected and ascended as our "first-fruits." In the matter of significance and others, we must "run with endurance the race that is set before us, looking to Jesus, the founder and perfector of our faith, who . . . is seated at the right hand of the throne of God" (Heb. 12:2). Submission to God is the key to biblical significance and the center of Jesus' perfect example in his incarnation.

Paul provides a helpful synthesis on the contrast between pride and humility by reflecting the emphases of the Pentateuch, the rest of the Old Testament, and the Gospels. His teaching about the danger of pride and the need for humility in Philippi and Corinth was complemented by Peter and James. The New Testament authors warned about the divisiveness of pride in the churches. The matrix of Christology resurfaces with a focus on sacrificial service with humility of mind. Both Philippi and Corinth were proud cities and illustrate the powerful effect that culture exerts on Christian ethics. Paul presented "selfish ambition" and "vainglory" that threatened the unity of the church (Phil. 2). The example of Christ points to the lowliness of crucifixion. According to the biblical principle of God's exaltation of the humble, the ascended Messiah was honored with unsurpassable greatness. In the Christ hymn, humility is forcefully communicated as a communicable attribute of God, meaning that this attitude and lifestyle should characterize his people. God does not take away our need for significance, but he transforms needs into blessings as we allow him to live through us. The "name above every name" proved that the last will become first through his ascension. This should be a primary expectation in our ministries and our eschatological hope! Corinth illustrated the same warnings and needs even more vividly. The city was a center of pride and pleasures in the empire, and the quarreling church followed the culture in boasting about its members' prestige. Arrogant opponents attacked Paul, the character of Christ, and a cross-shaped humility with serious consequences. Paul responded that all relationships with God, both salvation and calling, were divine gifts and enablements; therefore, "Let him who boasts boast only in the Lord." Humility—not pride—is the proper credential for ministry, because God's power is made evident in our weakness.

Lessons of the Study

What has this analysis of the antithesis between pride and humility achieved? Its contribution can be seen in several ways. First, the topics have been explored frequently through world history in general and Christian thinking in particular. There is a universal recognition that pride and humility are foundational character traits in human living and the dynamics of personal and international relationships. But a careful analysis of the meaning and development of the concepts had been neglected. This study has attempted to enhance our understanding of what pride and humility mean and how they have been desirable or dangerous.

Second, most studies have explored the virtue and vice separately. This analysis, on the other hand, has attempted to juxtapose them so that they can mutually illumine each other. Other treatments have usually involved extrabiblical sources, which we summarized briefly in our Introduction. This study has emphasized biblical theology, which has been analyzed less frequently. I am not aware of others books with this emphasis.

Third, this project has changed my thinking about humility and pride. I began with a common understanding that was based on dictionary definitions. Humility is "a modest or low view of one's importance, rank, or abilities." In other words, according to dictionaries, it is self-depreciating. Ironically I had thought of humility (and pride) as a single, individual virtue (or vice) which, with discipline, could be analyzed, quantified, and developed (or repressed). With the classical/modern meaning, I gravitated toward a "worm theology." Sometimes I tried to be more humble than my peers, only to discover that I was proud to be so humble! If a low sense of oneself is a good defense against bullying competitors, is not the lowest sense better? Definitions of the biblical meaning are quick to specify that humility does not mean making oneself a doormat. We can recall from our Introduction earlier that humility is a virtue that is foreign to all ancient societies, who avoided it as degrading or servile. We can also recall that it has been rejected in modernity as well, an era that has been characterized by an insatiable will to power. I was surprised to learn that pride and humility were reversed in modernity; humility became a vice, while pride has become a virtue. So, how do we apply teachings of Christ that are so countercultural? One of the most difficult aspects of this study is that Jesus turned the world's view of greatness on its head. It was a great reversal in which "the last become the first" in God's kingdom!

Pride, as a desirable attitude of successful living, is easier to think about because it is pervasive in our sinful world. It is easy to rationalize, when everyone around us approaches life in a self-interested way. Scholars in Christian traditions have agreed that pride as self-centeredness is the human condition. It is usually defined as "a satisfaction that is derived from one's achievements or qualities that are widely admired; a sense of one's own dignity and worth." Pride is generally valued, but no one, ancient or modern, likes a braggart—someone who makes us feel that they are superior to us and other people. No one on earth likes to be humiliated or denigrated.

I can now list four ways that the study has changed or refined my thinking. First, I no longer perceive humility as a single virtue that can be analyzed and quantified in isolation from other traits. In fact, humility has developed throughout history as two incompatible concepts. One is the classical and modern notion of human character traits; a person is characteristically virtuous or vicious in a variety of social behaviors. Humanistic concepts are inadequate for biblical realities, because the Bible never separates a person's character from his or her standing before God and his people, whether in truth or error. The Creator is central to understanding pride and humility in the Bible.

How should we define the concepts and their contrast? Interestingly, we search in vain for a thorough biblical analysis of pride or humility, although the various aspects of our study have been mentioned in the many sources that we have consulted. At the most basic level, the Bible defines humility as God-centeredness and pride as self-centeredness. The latter trait is not selfishness per se, but rather an orientation away from God toward willful rebellion and disobedience. The etymology of humility is derived from *humus* ("earthy"), with a backward glance to the creation of humanity from the earth, inbreathed by the breath of God (Gen. 2:7).

We were made creatures to be nurtured by our Maker. Philip Yancey concurs with this conclusion in the following remark: "As theologian Daniel Hawks puts it, 'The basic human problem is that everyone believes that there is a God and I am it.' . . . Humility means that in the presence of God I gain a glimpse of my true state in the universe, which exposes my smallness at the same time it reveals God's greatness."[1] Jon Bloom is also on target: "Humility is essentially the recognition of what is real—simply assessing things as they really are. To be fully humble is to fully trust God (Proverbs 3:5) who is the Truth (John 14:6; 17:17); to govern according to his just ways and perfect work (Deuteronomy 32:4); and to be content with what he gives us (Hebrews 13:5), knowing that 'a person cannot receive even one thing unless it is given him from heaven' (John 3:27)."[2] This God-centered understanding of humility is obviously absent from the secular passions of the world.

The concepts are usually used in clusters of similar characteristics and effects. Humility as lowliness under God occurs in connection with concepts like obedience, dedication, service,

---

1. Philip Yancey, *Prayer: Does It Make Any Difference?* (Grand Rapids: Zondervan, 2006), 37.
2. Jon Bloom, "Don't Let Pride Steal Your Joy!," *Revive* 46, 2 (2015): 14.

or love for God and others. So when believers are exhorted to "seek humility," they are to "seek the LORD, all you humble of the land, . . . who do his just commands" (Zeph. 2:3). This is a turning from pride and idols toward a renewed dedication to the true worship of God (cf. Deut. 8:2–3). Pride as presumptuous boasting occurs in conjunction with oppression, rebellion, idolatry, and factiousness. These clusters of sin should not obscure that pride and humility have been viewed as antithetical foundations of religious ethics. All of this means that the virtue and the vice describe the character of the whole person in a social context. We cannot say that a person is humble or proud without including the effects of their character on social circumstances and relationships.

Second, the concepts may be personal traits, but they are strongly social and communal. I was surprised to discover that humility of mind, a Christ-centered attitude, is biblically imperative for unity in the church. Having been frequently involved in conflict resolution, I can testify that this is true in a practical sense. It is literally true! If Christ is not given highest priority in Christian work, then the members will begin to quarrel and fight over the "best way to serve." This makes sense when we learn that we should consider no gift as superior to others under God (1 Cor. 12), and we should esteem the interests of other believers as more important than our own (Phil. 2). Comparisons and competitions in the church create conflicts and are manifestations of pride that generate quarrels and godless detours.

Third, I uncovered the valuable insight that pride at its core is competitive. A proud person gets no pleasure from personal position or possessions unless they make that person feel superior to others by comparison. Human nature naturally gravitates toward comparatives and superlatives in thinking about who is truly good or unspeakably evil. The prime possession is an illusion of self-sufficient power from status and wealth. Since the fall human pride has been the impossible and illicit desire to be as powerful and great as God—people blindly pursue it anyway. Proud people try to win at any cost and generate wars to be "like all the nations" (1 Sam. 8:5). Pride provokes some people to oppress and enslave others on an international scale. For personal advantage, pride is willing to betray or plunder friends and associates. In spite of the danger of broken relationships, it condones infidelity simply because some people feel entitled to have what they want without consequences. But apart from God, standards disappear. God responds with judgment, "so that they will know that I am the sovereign Lord." God has allowed pride so that its vanity can underscore his justice in judging the self-destructiveness of futile ambitions.

Fourth, in contrast, I have learned that we cannot categorize humility and pride as virtue and vice respectively. This adjustment is similar to the first change in my thinking. "Virtue" has been historically understood as human behavior that reflects high moral standards; it is moral excellence that promotes individual and collective uprightness and greatness. Classically, it was derived from *vir* ("manliness") and the Middle English *virtu* (with a similar nuance from the thirteenth century). It refers to a human quality without theological implications. Likewise, "vice" is human behavior or a habit that is socially considered to be degrading, immoral, or evil without connection to the Bible. Biblical theology forbids the advantages of noble birth (in the past) or "genetic superiority" (in the present) in assessing godly character. Nothing from achievement—to wealth, to rank, or to prestige—can stand before the perfections of God. In fact, achievements usually promote our pride or blind us to our need for the Lord. Everyone "by their unrighteousness suppresses the truth" (cf. Rom. 1:18). Besides, the great reversals in history and the Gospels mean that pride and humility are valued differently by Christ and secular cultures. This means that traits like humility are rooted in submission to God and then service for others' needs.

Biblical humility (or loving submission to God) focuses our lives on him and draws us away from the lesser things—temporal and transitory—that haunt our days on earth. It cannot be quantified and probably cannot be proven in this world. Various Christian thinkers have pondered about how we can recognize humble people. Augsburger puts it this way, "Humility, the tangible evidence that one loves God with heart, soul, strength, and mind is visible to others, but not so visible to the self."[3] Augsburger's point is that someone who loves others out of their affection for God is radically different from the survival-of-the-fittest ethos around us. But he alludes that a truly humble person is not self-obsessed. Lewis noted that we can recognize a humble person, because "He will not be thinking about humility: he will not be thinking about himself at all."[4] In Paul's words, "I have been crucified with Christ. It is no longer I who live, but Christ who lives in me" (Gal. 2:20).

The arrogant Corinthians made themselves judges of Paul's ministry. At first Paul cared little "that I should be judged by you or by any human court. In fact, I do not even judge myself" (1 Cor. 4:3). This means that humble believers judge only in the Lord according to his Word. It also means that humble people are too busy serving God to be introspectively concerned about their status. "For I am not aware of anything against myself," he continued, "but I am not thereby acquitted. It is the Lord who judges me" (v. 4). In other words, Paul knew of nothing in his ministry that required an apology. Biblical humility is inseparable from accountability before God. Paul would eventually

3. David Augsburger, *Dissident Discipleship: A Spirituality of Self-Surrender, Love of God, and Love of Neighbor* (Grand Rapids: Brazos, 2006), 122.
4. C. S. Lewis, *Mere Christianity* (1952; repr., San Francisco: HarperSanFrancisco, 1952), 128.

list his credentials that made him the greatest missionary and minister who ever lived. But he did not live to seek greatness on earth, and he knew that his weakness channeled God's strength through his faithfulness.

Therefore, I would conclude that the Bible teaches that true humility is real in the Holy Spirit. Humanity in general, on the other hand, pursues an elusive and transitory ideal, prioritizing its power, wealth, and strength. One should not equate meekness with God as a human virtue—it is a divinely enabled character trait. Human virtue is servile, while the latter is worthy of exaltation and greatness. Paul exhorted the Corinthians to boast only in the Lord. So we should say, "I have significance because God has worked through my submission to his will." In view of this disparity, we must conclude that people have some sense of the ideal of humility. But humanity in general has concluded that it is elusive in the real pressures of our prideful world. Most people seek the approval and applause of the world rather than the glory of God.

Fifth, related to the above, I have learned that the social image of humility is weakness and passivity. For this reason, it has not been respected or desired in ancient and modern societies that favor heroic significance and security. Regrettably, some Christians, like the Corinthians, have followed suit. One Internet site, which will remain unnamed, defined biblical humility as "a quality of being courteously respectful of others; it is the opposite of aggressiveness." I have learned that biblical humility is "aggression for God" that elevates us from our limitations and shortcomings. Jesus was not passive when, as the Son of God, he embraced his incarnation and "for the joy that was set before him endured the cross, despising the shame, and is seated at the right hand of the throne of God" (Heb. 12:2).

In conclusion, why should we seek this humility in the Spirit for which saints have suffered so greatly through the ages? The simple answer is that this is the way of wise living, godly significance, and eternal meaning in a dying world. Moses, "who was more humble than anyone else on earth," enjoyed special intimacy with God. But few people have desired to know God "face-to-face" (Num. 12:1–8). Hannah was reviled for her barrenness. In spite of her circumstances, she kept on praying to the Lord. God gave her one of the greatest prophets and king-makers in Israel's history. Hannah celebrated by singing, "Talk no more so very proudly, let not arrogance come from your mouth. . . . The LORD makes poor and makes rich; he brings low and he exalts . . . for not by might shall a man prevail" (1 Sam. 2:3, 7, 9). Joseph could have boasted for a long time without pause, but he humbly comforted his family, "You meant evil against me, but God meant it for good, to bring it about that many people should be kept alive, as they are today" (Gen. 50:20). With an echo of Hannah's praise, Mary accepted the incredible gift and responsibility of mothering the Messiah. "Let it be to me according to your word" (Luke 1:38). Then she sang, "My spirit rejoices in God my Savior, for he has looked on the humble estate of his servant. . . . He has scattered the proud in the thoughts of their hearts; he has brought down the mighty from their thrones and exalted those of humble estate" (vv. 47, 51–52). The list goes on from Genesis to Revelation! We should seek humility because it is the heart of our self-giving God, the character of Christ, and the promise of exaltation now and in the future.

Questions for Discussion

1. Are humility and pride traits that can be analyzed and quantified in isolation?
2. Why does the modern reversal of pride as a virtue make ministry especially difficult?

3. Does the Bible avoid careful definitions of pride and humility, requiring that readers formulate their own thinking? Or are the biblical narratives clear and vivid in their understanding of these traits?
4. How does the limitless greatness of God expose the necessity of humility in believers' lives?
5. Why are our social contexts so important in understanding pride and humility?
6. Why has God allowed the human condition of pride to continue through history? Why doesn't he punish it so severely that people choose a humble lifestyle even if they do not want to?
7. Why should we not think of humility and pride as virtue and vice respectively? Why must all believers seek humility in the Spirit?
8. What is the social image of humility, and why is it inaccurate?

Further Reading

Derber, Charles. *The Pursuit of Attention: Power and Ego in Everyday Life*. Second edition. Oxford: Oxford University Press, 2000. This is not a work of biblical theology. Instead it focuses on the pervasiveness of pride in the dynamics of the contemporary world, under the headings "Individualism," and "The Power of Status."

Glossary

antithetical. Opposite.

Aphrodite. The Greek goddess of fertility and beauty (the Roman Venus).

automatic. In anthropology, an innate or intuitive response to circumstances.

autonomy. The assumption that an individual is free to make judgments and decisions apart from outside authorities (such as God).

braggadocio. Boasting with swagger and pretention.

bravado. Boastfulness or bragging about one's accomplishments or character.

censorial. Judgmental assessment of content that is objectionable to moral standards, usually involving punishment.

chaos. The effect of sin on the orders of creation as represented biblically by dragons and monsters (Leviathan).

cherub. Angelic guardians of God's glory (cf. Ezek. 1; 10).

childlike. Powerless.

city. In the Bible, the organized gathering of unbelievers to find security apart from God.

covenant. An arrangement for relationship between God and humanity, initiated by God.

criterion. A standard by which a judgment is made.

Day Star. A title of a king who is believed to be the hope of the world (cf. Acts 12:21–23).

depravity. The universal condition of sinful humanity.

discipleship. A synonym for mentoring or investing in the training of believers.

divine assembly. In the ancient world, pagan religions believed in an assembly of gods who would determine the affairs of the world.

ecclesial. Pertaining to church matters.

Enlightenment. The European movement in the seventeenth and eighteenth centuries that emphasized reason and autonomy rather than tradition and revelation.

face. An Old Testament metaphor for presence, as in Moses' face-to-face encounters with God.

gates. Passageways for transportation and trade.

God-centeredness. A concern for submission to God in all of life's circumstances, or "lov[ing] the Lord your God with all your heart and with all your soul and with all you mind" (Matt. 22:37).

heart. In the Bible this stands for the center or identity of the person and the matrix for thinking about our place in family and society. The equivalent today is the brain as the biological center of the person.

Hellenism. The culture of ancient Greece.

hubris. An exaggerated sense of self, generally synonymous with pride.

humility of mind. Absence of conceit and selfish ambition; an aggressive concern for the interests of others.

idol. An object of worship other than the Trinitarian God.

ignominious. Disgraceful, humiliating.

image. A representation of a person that suggests their character.

imago Dei. The essential significance of a human person as created by God, supremely of the incarnate Jesus Christ.

insolence. Rudeness, impudence.

intuitive. Instinctive acceptance of truth without conscious reasoning.

invincibility. Incapable of being defeated.

king. In the ancient world, beyond an individual ruler, a corporate representative of the people accountable to God.

labyrinth. A metaphor for the complexity of life that obscures God-pleasing living.

land of blessing. God's promise of a land for Israel that would be their home.

lowly, last. A willingness to be insignificant in the world as opposed to "royalty."

Most High. A title for God that exalts him as greater than everything.

mountains, seas. As metaphors, the dwelling places of the gods.

mythical. Concepts or ideas that are characteristic of cultures, often concerning idealized values.

name. In the Bible the identity, character, and reputation of a person.

natural philosophy. The belief that only natural laws and forces operate in the world as opposed to transcendent or supernatural forces such as God.

oppressors. Proud people who take advantage of others for personal gain.

paradigm. A model of how something or someone should be understood.

Pentateuch. The first five books of the Bible, the books of Moses, the Torah.

perseverance. Holding to a course or direction in life with steadfastness.

pompous. High-sounding, bombastic words and behavior to parade one's self-importance.

poor. "Poor [humble] in spirit" rather than poverty in property from laziness or reckless living.

prescient. Foresight of actions or events before they occur.

presumptuous. Arrogant attitude or behavior.

principle. A basic truth or foundational standard in the system of beliefs.

promise. In the case of God, an assurance that will come to pass.

prototypical. An original example on which later examples are based or judged.

psalms of lament. The cries of believers to God for deliverance from godless persecutors.

ransom. Redemptive payment to release believers from imprisonment to sin.

reflexive. An action with self as both subject and object.

revélation. Knowledge given by God.

self-centeredness. More than selfishness, the prioritizing of self in the circumstances of life, a self-sufficiency in living with no regard for God.

servant-leadership. An eagerness to serve, "not lording it over those entrusted to you" (1 Peter 5:3).

Shaddai. God Almighty as sovereign of the earth.

significance. Worthy of attention, social importance.

sin. An act or condition of breaking divine law, especially religious as distinct from evil.

supercilious. Showing arrogant disdain for another person.

theocracy. The governance of Israel by God.

vainglory. A futile delusion of one's own worth, with little to no thought of God.

vengeance. Inflicting harm on unjust adversaries.

vice. A human practice or habit that characterizes evil, degrading, or immoral behavior.

vindication. To justify or support one's claim.

virtue. A human practice or habit that characterizes moral excellence or a beneficial character trait.

walk. A biblical metaphor for faithful dependence on God in daily details.

wisdom. The God-given skill of understanding how life should be lived.

Select Bibliography

Boa, Kenneth. *Conformed to His Image: Biblical and Practical Approaches to Spiritual Formation.* Grand Rapids: Zondervan, 2001.

Carter, Philippa. *The Servant-Ethic in the New Testament.* New York: Peter Lang, 1999.

Cooper, Terry D. *Sin, Pride & Self-Acceptance: The Problem of Identity in Theology & Psychology.* Downers Grove, IL: InterVarsity Press, 2003.

Derber, Charles. *The Pursuit of Attention: Power and Ego in Everyday Life.* 2nd ed. New York: Oxford University Press, 2000.

Kleinberg, Aviad M. *7 Deadly Sins: A Very Partial List.* Cambridge, MA: Belknap, 2008.

Konyndyk DeYoung, Rebecca. *Vainglory: The Forgotten Vice.* Grand Rapids: Eerdmans, 2014.

Lewis, C. S. *Mere Christianity.* Reprint, San Francisco: HarperSanFrancisco, 2001.

Morgan, Christopher W., and Robert Peterson, eds. *Fallen: A Theology of Sin.* Wheaton, IL: Crossway, 2013.

Murray, Andrew. *Humility.* Reprint, New Kensington, PA:

Whitaker House, 1982.

Pyne, Robert A. *Humanity and Sin: The Creation, Fall, and Redemption of Humanity*. Nashville: Word, 1999.

Ramm, Bernard L. *Offense to Reason: A Theology of Sin*. San Francisco: Harper & Row, 1985.

Savage, Timothy B. *Power through Weakness: Paul's Understanding of the Christian Ministry in 2 Corinthians*. SNTSMS, vol. 86.

Shuster, Marguerite. *The Fall and Sin: What We Have Become as Sinners*. Grand Rapids: Eerdmans, 2004.

Smith, David L. *With Willful Intent: A Theology of Sin*. Wheaton, IL: Bridgepoint, 1994.

Whitfield, Charles L., Barbara Whitfield, Russell Park, and Janeane Prevatt. *The Power of Humility: Choosing Peace Over Conflict in Relationships*. Deerfield Beach, FL: Health Communications, 2006.

Index of Scripture

Index of Subjects and Names

103–4, 121, 144, 150, 159,
183–84, 187, 192–93, 196,
199–200
and human condition, 9, 25, 28,
38, 64, 92, 115, 188, 193, 200
humiliation of, 45, 54, 58, 78,
80, 94, 98, 104, 110, 112, 115,
117, 130, 136, 162, 165–66,
186–88
importance of, 16, 44, 54, 69,
79, 85, 106, 122, 141, 144,
147, 157, 159, 179, 192, 204
and oppression, 65–66, 68–69,
106, 110, 187–88, 195
and self-centeredness, 11, 21,
24, 26, 52–53, 58, 139, 156,
159, 162, 183, 193–94, 204
and self-promotion, 10, 130,
157, 160
and vainglory, 51, 160, 179, 204
a vice (virtue), 1, 3, 5, 8, 10,
14–16, 20, 37, 41, 51, 139,
145, 149, 160, 181, 192, 195–
96, 200, 204
definition of, 13, 54, 149, 151
Pritchard, James, 108

Rand, Ayn, 11
reversal of values, 14, 20, 80, 82,
86, 90, 122, 128, 134–36, 145,
148, 150, 152, 168, 189–90,
193, 199

Ringer, Robert, 12
Ross, Allen, 32

Satan, 23, 28, 54, 58–60, 62, 65,
86, 102–3, 108, 110–11, 118,
177
Savage, Timothy, 169
Seth (and Enoch), 30–31, 110
significance, ix, 1, 2, 4, 16, 35,
37, 50–53, 84, 99, 111, 122,
131, 136, 150, 159, 162–64,
166, 175, 178, 184, 190–91,
198–99, 202, 204
Smick, Elmer, 62
Solomon, Robert, 9–10
Suchocki, Marjorie, 23

temptation, 23, 35, 38, 60, 95,
100–1, 103
Thompson, J. A., 49
Tongue, D. H., 43

Wenham, Gordon, 29
Westermann, Claus, 75
Wilkins, Michael, 124
Williams, A. J., 99
Wilson, Jonathan, 146

Yancey, Philip, 194
Young, E. J., 110, 115

Zimmerli, Walther, 96

More from P&R on sanctification

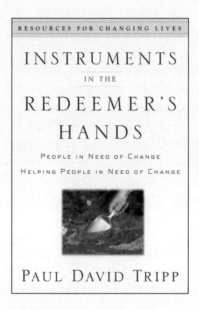

RESOURCES FOR CHANGING LIVES

INSTRUMENTS
IN THE
REDEEMER'S HANDS

PEOPLE IN NEED OF CHANGE
HELPING PEOPLE IN NEED OF CHANGE

PAUL DAVID TRIPP

Paul Tripp helps us discover where change is needed in our own lives and the lives of others. Following the example of Jesus, Tripp reveals how to get to know people at a deeper level, and how to lovingly speak truth to them without breaking fellowship.

"Helps us help others (and ourselves) by giving grace-centered hope that we can indeed change, and by showing us the biblical way to make change happen."
—**Skip Ryan**

"A wonderful application of the old Gaelic saying, 'God strikes straight blows with crooked sticks.' As inadequate as we are, God is eager to use us to help others change. The more you apply the biblical principles discussed in the book, the more readily you will fit into his mighty hand."
—**Ken Sande**

More from P&R on humility

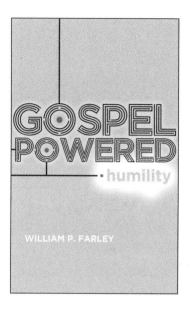

Humility, while essential for conversion and sanctification, may be the least emphasized virtue. Farley alerts us to the problem and shows how ours is a humbling gospel, stressing the need for a ministry that promotes humility.

"In *The Holiness of God*, R.C. Sproul says that the reason he wrote a book on holiness was a deep awareness of his own lack of holiness. Similarly, William Farley wrote this book out of an awareness of his lack of humility. Though in recent years we have witnessed the release of several excellent titles on this subject, *Gospel-Powered Humility* carefully grounds humility in the good news of the gospel. This is a book that will teach and convict every believer."
—**Tim Challies**, blogger, author, and social media consultant

More from P&R on sanctification

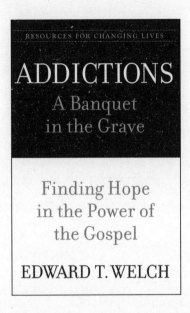

Scripture reveals addicts' true condition: like guests at a banquet thrown by "the woman Folly," they are already in the grave. (Prov. 9:13–18) Can we not escape our addictions? Following Jesus, we have "immense hope that God can give power so that we are no longer mastered by the addiction."

"Destroys the myth that addiction is a disease and sin is a sickness. Welch shows that the hopeless cycle of 'sickness, recovery, and relapse' must be replaced with the biblical view of sin, salvation, and sanctification. As a pastor, biblical counselor, and redeemed (not recovering) ex-heroin addict, I believe Welch has given every pastor, parishioner, and anyone caught in the bondage of idolatry/addiction a biblical road map to lasting freedom."
—**Peter Garich**, Dayspring Center for Biblical Counseling